You Were Shy?

from the Shadows to the Spotlight

Esther Stark

Dedication

To all who yearn…
to make a change…
to overcome your challenges…
to step beyond that which holds you back.

———

"Life isn't about finding yourself.
Life is about creating yourself."

-- George Bernard Shaw

Contents

Advance Praise for YOU Were Shy?

"This profoundly moving memoir weaves together one woman's shyness, persistence, and personal grief, as she explores how her experiences have shaped her relationships and sense of belonging. Esther's heartfelt story captures the essence of intimacy and connection, reminding us that even in our most vulnerable moments we can find strength and healing."

— Marjorie Lin Kyriopoulos, writer, editor, photographer, and author of *HeartStrings*, a memoir.

∞∞∞

"'You were shy?' I asked, incredulous to learn my friend had ever been anything but outgoing, confident, and engaged. Esther Stark's story of overcoming the shadow that defined her early years had me turning the pages as quickly as I could to uncover the secrets of her transformation."

— Joy Ng, author of *Quiet Courage - The True Story of a French World War II War Bride and her American Soldier* and *Even There, Love, Faith and Danger in Wild Alaska*.

Acknowledgements

To my sons Larry, Stephen, Christopher and Duane — From the moment you took your first breath, you've been an integral part of me. Your joy is my joy, your tears are my tears, and your pain is my pain. I'm constantly amazed by the unique individuals you've become; four distinct personalities shaped in the same loving environment. As your mother, my role has been to nurture, support, and guide you through life's journey. But what I've come to realize is that you've also been my pillars of strength, my confidants, and my teachers. As you grew into young men, there were times when you lifted me up when I couldn't stand alone. You may have outgrown my lap, but you'll never outgrow my love. You are forever etched in my heart, and I thank God every day for each one of you.

To my late husband John — We were young and naive but we spent 21 years together, a rollercoaster of adventures and challenges. You had more faith in me than I had in myself. Your audacious nature took us places that I would never have experienced, had it not been for you. I thank you for that. Gone way too soon, but not forgotten.

To my sister, Phyllis --- for putting up with my constant text messages, asking questions and picking your brain, clarifying many details of my early childhood memories.

To my husband Sean — I would never have started, or completed, this book without you. Your encouragement has been never ending. Your faith that I'd complete it steadfast.

You quietly slipped into the shadows, allowing me to guiltlessly spend countless hours, days, months in front of my computer while I worked on this book. Your love for me is the epitome of 1 Corinthians 13:4.

"Love is patient, love is kind. It does not envy, it does not boast, it is not proud. It does not dishonor others, it is not self-seeking, it is not easily angered, it keeps no record of wrong." 1 Cor 13:4

My dear friend Joy Ng — When Sean first suggested I write my story, you encouraged me and became a trustworthy mentor throughout the course of my writing. I am extremely thankful for the insights and contributions you have provided to make this book possible. You inspired me by publishing two of your own books: *Quiet Courage - The True Story of a French World War II War Bride and her American Soldier,* and also *Even There - Love, Faith, and Danger in Wild Alaska.*

To Marjorie Lin Kyriopoulos ---author of *HeartStrings*, I give a huge thank you for your valuable skills and the time you spent editing this book.

∞∞∞

Why I Wrote My Story

An Introduction

"There is no greater agony than bearing an untold story inside of you." -- Maya Angelou

I spent four decades of my life desperately wanting to join – to be a part of – the world that thrived around me. Instead, I hid in the shadows while I watched others take part in activities; laughing and enjoying life. I yearned to be like them.

YOU Were Shy? is a true story. It depicts my life of hiding in the shadows of fear until, at the age of 41, I was thrust into a world that forced me to make some changes. Changes that helped to pull me from the cruel pit of guilt and grief, and helped me navigate the struggles of shyness that threatened to suffocate me.

It's a story of triumph where, by taking one step at a time, this shy, broken, docile woman stepped out of the shadows and into life's spotlight — becoming a confident artist, teacher, singer, and author.

I smile at people's reactions when I mention my shyness.

"YOU were shy?" Shocked expressions question me.

"Yes. Painfully shy." My head nods.

A wise person once said,

"The time we have already lived we can't change, but it doesn't define us. We can extend that lifeline and make choices of what is going to happen in our future. We can look at our past and decide what changes we would like to make. We can learn lessons from past experiences. We can make a choice to take one step at a time to change the things that we would like to change."

If this deeply personal and emotional story of trials and triumph can help one person realize their past does not define them; that they can overcome the challenges they face; that they can start new today and become the person they want to be; then every minute I spend on this book, every raw story I've shared, is worthwhile.

Before I was forced to take that first step in 1992, I only dreamed of living outside of my shadows. I believe you too can make a change, and become the person you want to be. **I challenge you to give it a try... starting today.**

No matter who you are, no matter what you've done, no matter where you come from, you can always make a change to be a better version of yourself.

∞ ∞ ∞

Part One - The Catalyst

Chapter One

Will You Be Ok?

"Will you be ok?" His voice, filled with compassion, squelched any intimidation I may have otherwise felt by the badge pinned to the breast of his brown uniform. He stood at the door, waiting for my reply. I hadn't asked myself that question yet, or even considered it. I still muddled through the fog of my brain each day, struggling to accomplish the tasks at hand. I nodded yes, my voice silenced by the lump in my throat. My thoughts drifted back to that night only weeks before.

"Stay in the car, Chris!" Flashing lights lit up the dark sky on March 1, 1992. I flung open the car door. My sister stopped me in the yard as I raced toward the house. Her thin, bony arms grasped me tight, her sobs hysterical.

"You can't go in, Esther." Her tightened clench pulled me against her trembling body, her shoulder muffled the scream that escaped my throat.

Chris! My thoughts returned to him. I shot a panic-stricken glance back to the car just in time to see him burying his anguished face in his hands, his body rocking back and forth. Witnessing my reaction told him what he didn't want to know.

Less than an hour earlier, the kitchen was filled with the sweet, chocolaty aroma of fresh baked brownies. Our family's favorite cookbook, made many years earlier in grade school by my eldest son, lay open to the batter-stained page, identifying the repeated use of the brownie recipe. Chris, our 15 year-old son, had just pulled a hot batch from the oven.

Brownies or chocolate chip cookies are two treats I can't resist. I could devour an entire pan, along with a half-gallon of milk, in one evening. The temptation of the brownies had been hastened this evening by the knot in my stomach. A knot that grew tighter by the hour. My husband, John, had moved into a cottage one mile away. We needed some space from one another. He called often. Today was no exception. Once to continue our discussion of the financial burden of two households versus one. He called again saying my sister, Mary, would be stopping by his house that evening. He was the editor of the Community Connection newsletter, published by a local handicap nonprofit organization. He planned to help Mary with an article she had written for the newsletter. Then, a third call. The one causing my stomach to flip flop, tightening into a hard ball, refusing to settle down.

"I'm cleaning my guns so I can sell them. You might remind Steve he needs to clean his gun too, since he was out shooting last week."

"I'll tell him." Every nerve in my body bristled, the hair raising to attention, as I hung up the phone. The pounding in my chest, deafening to my ears. My mind quickly scoured the conversation, searching for the unspoken words that lingered in the air... the echo of threats or a cry for help?

You're jumping to conclusions, Esther. This is his way of manipulating you. I tried putting my nagging fear at ease. *Ignore the call. He's fine!*

The evening had been pleasant prior to that phone call. The warmth of the low-burning pellet stove, combined with the sweet smell from the kitchen, gave this otherwise chilly March evening a cozy feel. Our two youngest sons, Chris and Duane, were at home. Our two oldest sons, Larry and Stephen, on dates. Fourteen-year-old Duane, still wrapped in a towel from his recent shower, chatted on the telephone. Me, not being able to calm my fears, decided to check on John.

"I'm going to take some brownies to your dad."

"He'll like these," Chris said, smiling as he helped me place several warm brownies on a plate. I knew I wasn't going to rest until I reassured myself that my mind was needlessly running amuck.

We had one land line phone, and four teenage sons. Our household policy: if a call-waiting came in for one of us, they got off the phone. As I wrapped aluminum foil over the plate, Duane stuck his head in the kitchen doorway, scrunched brows highlighting the concern in his voice.

"Aunt Mary is on the phone and she's crying." *Mary is supposed to be working with John this evening.* My pulse quickened.

"Mary?" My voice squeaked as I answered the phone.

"You better get down here!" her pause seemed unending as she struggled to say the words through her sobs.

"John's been shot!"

"Chris come with me, your dad's been shot!" I dropped the phone. All logic crumbled into a million pieces. I rushed out the door with Chris, leaving a wide eyed, 14 year-old standing alone in his wet towel. It seemed only minutes before Duane,

Stephen and his girlfriend, René, showed up at John's cottage. I have no recollection of talking with an officer. The kids took me home. Larry, with his girlfriend, arrived at the house soon after. Stephen made the necessary phone calls to John's family.

A mattress thrown on the floor next to Stephen's bed is where I slept that night. I couldn't bear to sleep alone in my bedroom. I wanted to hold each of my sons in my arms, never letting go.

Several weeks later, the doorbell rang. A Sheriff's deputy introduced himself.

"I wanted to check on you." His soft voice exhibited genuine concern. "I was on call the night of your husband's death." He hesitated as if contemplating what else he should say. His next sentence faded into a fog. Then he asked again, "Will you be ok?" He stepped closer. A light touch on my shoulder and his gentle smile conveyed the silent words, *I understand,* when I couldn't speak. He returned to his patrol car. The gravel crunched beneath the tires. The hum of the engine faded. I remained still as his words echoed in my mind.

"Will you be ok?"

The struggle you're in today is developing the
strength you need for tomorrow.

∞ ∞ ∞

LPN to KFC

"**W**e have an opening. Come over and apply for the job. I'll put in a good word for you." Cody said.

My father worked the swing shift. My homemaker mother didn't drive until I was in high school. Driving this country girl 18 miles to a job, then picking her up later was not feasible. Plus, my mother refused to drive after dark. At age 19, and out of school, I moved in with my older sister, Phyllis, and her family. She managed an apartment complex with her husband in Federal Way, Washington. One of their tenants, Cody, worked across the street as Assistant Manager of the Kentucky Fried Chicken (KFC).

Sunny skies were deceiving on this chilly March day. I pulled my long, thick hair in front of my shoulders, running a comb through to the ends. A light flip of my head moved the brunette strands back into place, cascading down to my lower back. Blue eye shadow lined my lids, with black cat-eye liner above the upper lashes, in the 1970 fashionable style. I applied the final touch of mascara… waterproof is always a necessity for me.

During my senior year of high school I mentioned to my parents that I wanted to be a Licensed Practical Nurse (LPN). Soon after, a full set of medical encyclopedias arrived at our house. I suspect in their minds if I studied the encyclopedias, I would be able to get a job as an LPN. With eight siblings my elder, they were excited that I might finish high school, the first in the family. In 1968, college was a luxury not a necessity; a luxury I knew they couldn't afford. I never asked, nor did I have a clue how to apply for, or the courage to approach a school counselor, about financial aid. The dream died.

Here I was looking for a job in Washington. After changing several outfits, I settled on a neatly pressed blouse and my bell bottom, polyester pants. I double checked the full-length mirror, approving my appearance. I patted my sweaty palms against my pant legs before crossing the busy street. *It's just an interview, Esther!* I swallowed hard and took a deep breath.

With the energy of a puppy, a teenage employee, dressed in a red and white candy-striped skirt and white blouse, came bouncing from the kitchen to greet me.

"Good morning." Her voice sounded chipper as she picked up a pen. "What can I get for you today?"

"Hi, I'm Esther. I was told you have an opening. I'd like to fill out an application."

"Oh, yes!" She waved her hand in a motion for me to follow her. "Come on in."

Maybe Cody did put in a good word for me. She seemed to be expecting me. I followed her into the kitchen. She didn't give me an application form. A loud *Whoosh* drew my attention to the massive cooker billowing hot plumes of steam as the lid opened. It filled the room with the aroma of original KFC chicken. I followed her to the back of the kitchen. The stainless-steel countertops glistened. Only a small bit of flour lay scattered on the floor beneath the breading machine of an otherwise spotless kitchen. At the back of the room, dressed in dark slacks, a white short sleeved shirt, and a black KFC bow tie, stood a tall, slender man. She introduced me.

"John, this is Esther. She's here about the job." She walked away. John glanced up. The corners of his full lips curved into a quick smile as he nodded hello. He returned his focus back to the torch in his hand and the equipment on which he worked.

I flinched at the loud *Poof*. A blast of red, yellow, and blue flame shot out of the torch. My eyes darted toward his left hand. I felt a pinch of disappointment at the sight of a ring. His voice snapped me back to attention. My face flushed. I hoped he hadn't seen my inquiry. My body rocked back and forth in a nervous gesture. His hazel eyes glanced my way for a split second, either oblivious to my awkwardness or unconcerned. With his focus back on the torch, he threw out questions; I responded.

"I worked a short time as a waitress and I've cashiered." My employment history was sparse at best. Silence. My insecurities magnified. Each pause, like a breeze to a candle, flickered my hopes.

"I learn fast." I felt a necessity to break the silence between questions. My employment history consisted of a waitress job that lasted two weekends due to the lack of transportation. Once I had my drivers license I was hired at a cabinet shop. I left at lunch time on the first day. I'd sorted screws for four hours. I never returned, not even for my paycheck. One summer I sold tickets for carnival rides at $40 per week. As I awaited John's next question, I heard my mother's voice.

"Don't set your goals so high then get disappointed when you can't do it." I'm sure she meant to protect me from disappointments as I talked about my goals. My interpretation: *Your goals are too high Esther, you'll never reach them.* I began to believe those words – again – as I stood in this interview. Like a frightened animal, trapped, I wanted to run. There was no escape. I'd have to finish the interview. My nervous gaze darted around the room, glad he focused on his torch and not at me. I bit my lip to stop the quiver. I can't cry. Tears had a way of sneaking out at undesirable times, when I was upset, nervous or embarrassed.

Pop! The torch startled me as it shut off; the flame withdrew. He set it aside. His eyes met mine as he smiled,

"Show up tomorrow at nine. We'll start your training then."

"I'll be here!"

A dream is an idea without a plan.
A goal is a dream with a plan.

∞ ∞ ∞

Now or Never

"Ok. Got it." I gave a nervous chuckle to lighten the impact of the reprimand.

"Do you think it was funny?" He scowled, the glare from the hazel eyes I'd previously admired bore through me like a bolt of lightning.

"No... no, I didn't think it was funny." I clenched my jaw to stop the quiver. John was an excellent, but stern, teacher. I was in, or near, tears more often than I could count. If I had to be shown a second time how to do something, I learned a silent nod would be my best response. Anything else might elicit an emotional scene on my part.

I placed a dab of White Shoulders perfume on my wrists before I sprinted out the door for work. The sweetness of the floral scent made me feel pretty. I'd never been confident about my appearance, so I took extra steps to look my best. My smiles were always hidden behind a cupped hand. I didn't want another experience like the one in high school when the puzzled expression of a classmate, who stared at my face, made me uncomfortable.

"What?" I asked, feeling vulnerable with this face-to-face encounter.

"I never noticed before. You have buck teeth!" I couldn't speak. I froze for a split second then made my way out of the room. Mortified, I stood trembling in the bathroom. I leaned close to the mirror. I wasn't aware I had buck teeth. Now I knew.

The morning sunshine hinted that Spring had arrived. It energized my night-owl body, in spite of the early hour. I resisted the urge to skip across the street to work. I grabbed my apron from a nearby hook as I entered the back door, tying it firmly around my waist. The night crew did a good job, I noted. As usual, the stainless steel shined, the floors spotless. John insisted on a clean-as-you-go policy. The store's appearance reflected that policy. I walked to John's office where I poked my head in the open doorway.

"Good morning, John." I said in a cheerful voice. John wrinkled his nose. He swiped his hand in front of a sour expression.

"I could smell you coming a mile away!" He turned back to his bookwork.

In the bathroom, I stifled the tears with tissue gently held to my eyes. I didn't want to destroy my make up. I scrubbed my wrists, inhaled a deep breath and went to my work station. When John came into the kitchen, I made as little conversation as possible.

John ran a strict store. The monthly profit and loss statement, and his bonuses proved it. His employees knew where they stood with him. He said what he thought, with little tact. He held back no reprimand, nor did he hold back praise for a job well done. Employees either admired him or considered him a real ass. Many employees who adhered to his strict discipline went on to be successful managers and supervisors. Likewise, in spite of many tears, my work ethic became top notch. I soon advanced to Assistant Manager, and later Manager.

In high school my closest friends were guys. I never understood the reason why. That trait has carried throughout my life. Since this was my norm, the friendship I developed with John through our work didn't seem out of the ordinary.

Many mornings John would arrive at work distraught. Over time he shared bits and pieces of his turmoil. His wife talked of divorce. He worried he would lose his infant son if that happened.

October's chilly air turned the leaves to brilliant fall colors. My apartment was lightly decorated with autumn decor. After a few paychecks, I rented one of the apartments that my sister managed. I enjoyed the independence of living on my own for the first time. My radio played the 70's top hits. I carried my steaming cup of tea upstairs, the cinnamon stick I used to stir it, still in the cup, filling the air with the aroma of fall. As I set the cup on the nightstand, a loud, rapid *Bang Bang Bang* on my door startled me, splashing liquid over the stand. The urgent pounding sent a wave of panic through me. *Something must be wrong!* I rushed down the stairs, feet sliding over the carpet. I expected to see a frantic sister standing at my door when I flung it open. Instead, I saw John, the color drained from his face. He looked frightened, devastated. He blurted out his story as he stood in the doorframe. His wife filed for divorce, took their baby boy and moved to California. His eyes stared deep into mine as if he were searching for something. His voice tightened as he fought to stay in control. He waved his hand in a quick gesture at himself, then toward me, then back at himself.

"It's now or never!"

The idea that John and I would ever become a couple was lightyears away from me. He was my boss. We never took our friendship outside the workplace, keeping it strictly platonic. I can only assume John's actions were out of determination to grasp hold of something when he thought he was losing everything.

Why I packed up my belongings that night and went with

him, I have no idea. Maybe I didn't know how to say no to an ultimatum. Maybe subconsciously I wanted to take a risk for once in my life. Maybe I anticipated that if I didn't go, I may, as so often in my life, be missing another opportunity. Maybe I didn't think at all. Maybe I just reacted.

*Life is about choices. Some we regret, some we're
proud of, some will haunt us forever.*

∞ ∞ ∞

Me and John - April 1971

Chapter Two

The House Across the Creek

The weathered old bridge groaned of age as the car creeped slowly across. A three-bedroom, wood-shingled house sat nestled near the hillside, across the creek. The home was built 13 miles out of town, by my father. It now bore the appearance of a tiny shack, worn with age.

It would be unlikely that Verdie Nelson, also known as Peach, would tip the scale at a 100 pounds soaking wet. Her 5'2" thin body is not what you would imagine of someone who'd given birth to nine children, birthed a stillborn baby girl, lost a three-month premature baby boy, and had two miscarriages. By the age of 38, Peach was done bearing children… she thought. By now she had a two-year-old granddaughter. Pregnant once again, she wondered if she had enough energy, or love, for one more baby. Peach shared her story with me.

"I couldn't bear the thought of another baby. I was tired. I had a grandchild." She lowered her head, hiding her pale blue-gray eyes as she continued, "I hid in the bedroom… I straightened a metal coat hanger and inserted it inside me… I tried to abort the pregnancy… It didn't work," she said between sniffles. She raised her head with an apologetic look. "But later I was glad it didn't work! I didn't think I could raise another baby." On October 6, 1950, she gave birth to a little girl. She named her Esther. Peach did muster up the energy to love that baby, and my baby sister two years later.

I have vague but fond memories of my early childhood. My sisters and I shared a bath in a laundry tub my mother would drag in from the back porch. Wrapped in a towel, we cuddled next to the wood stove where we would warm ourselves, allowing our wet hair to dry by the heat of a crackling fire. Our house always had the scent of rising yeast dough, followed by the smell of fresh baked bread. My mother served bread and butter with every meal.

My siblings and I would throw boards against the blackberry vines that lined our long driveway. The boards served as a ladder so we could reach the berries toward the top... the ones ripened by the hot summer sun... the plump ones... the ones filled with sweet juice... juice that oozed as we plucked the berry from the vine. We arrived back at the house with dry blood streaks on our arms and legs, with remnants of the berry thorns just under the surface of the skin. Our purple lips and fingers were evidence that not all the berries reached the gallon Crisco buckets.

Out back, a dirt path led to our luxury, two-seater outhouse: one seat for adults, one sized for children, always stocked with newspapers, catalogs or old magazines. On occasion, a corn cob hung from the ceiling, evidence of our father's sense of humor. A three-pound Folgers coffee can was placed under the foot of our bed for use in the middle-of-the-night.

Slate Creek birthed my love for water. Hours were spent in the creek on hot summer days. My older siblings taught me to swim, with awkward overhand strokes. My mother, after watching her father nearly drown when she was a little girl, had a fear of the water. She never got in but she encouraged us kids so that we didn't share the same fear. Innertubes carried us over the ripples and downstream. Then we carried the tubes back upstream to repeat the process. Several times I had the courage to jump from the tattered old bridge into the deepest part of the swimming hole — always with the help of a brother or sister's push as they yelled *"Jump!"*

My father's fingers were yellowed from nicotine. Born in Nebraska in 1903, the eldest of 13 children, his rough hands were evidence of years of labor intensive work as a logger, a carpenter, and a county road employee. When not on the job, he worked in his garage or gardened in our yard. He quit school after third grade I was told, yet he was an avid reader. I'd see him read the daily newspaper cover to cover. He read and collected western paperbacks.

His right thumb had been sawn off at the base of the nail. An accident during his carpentry years. As an adult, a visit with him never went without a game of checkers or backgammon. Nor did it go without my mother cooking her tangy sweet and sour ribs, or her moist Dream Whip syrup cake, at the request of my father. He knew those were my favorites. I enjoyed those grown-up visits with him. The conversations, the interactions, the ones we never had in my childhood or teen years. Working the swing shift meant I didn't see much of my father when I lived at home.

My mother, born in Little Rock, Arkansas in 1911, traveled, as an infant, in a peach basket on a train ride with her mother. The endearing nickname of Peaches — later shortened to Peach — stuck with her. I was in sixth grade before I learned Peach was only a nickname. Pulling my mother's paisley print dress around me became routine when company arrived. If I couldn't see them they couldn't see me. I didn't know what I was afraid of. My siblings greeted company with hugs. I often heard my mother say, "She's *SHY.*"

At school, there were days when I'd cling to my teacher's legs resisting her encouragement to join the children playing. I wanted to, but something stopped me. I watched from afar, alone, more than I joined.

The word *SHY* is often used lightly. It is so much more than a short, three letter word. It's a powerful word that can shape, can control, a person's entire life.

A Tiny Word — a World of Longings

———

The old Madrone tree towers in that yard across the creek to this day. In summer, the thin, reddish-brown bark peels away from the trunk and falls to the ground. It curls into, what we pretended to be, long, slender, Swisher Sweet Cigars. Cigars were the epitome of cool and glamor in the 1950's. Smoking was considered an act of elegance and sophistication. After we checked the curled bark for hidden earwigs, we dangled them, like cigars, from our lips... or held them between two fingers while we blew invisible smoke rings. Our cigars were classier than the candy cigarettes we could purchase from the store. When the bark peels away from the tree, the trunk is left with a smooth, soft surface; perfect for us to carve our initials.

Well over 60 years have elapsed since I lived in that house across the creek. My sisters and I have visited the creekside property on occasion. A rotted piece of rooftop lay in crumbles next to a small, rusted piece of mesh wire; the only remnants of the large cage which housed the chipmunks our father rescued while employed at the Oregon Caves.

Memories linger of that long ago swimming hole, now almost unrecognizable. The bank has changed, the rocks have shifted. The water of Slate Creek has become shallow. It ripples slowly around the protruding rocks. The old bridge is gone, replaced many years ago to the far end of the property. A fragment of tarnished metal crumbled in my hand as I picked it up. It was the only visible sign of the cabin, built by my father for my oldest sister, Ruth, and her husband, Ernie. I never liked Ernie… and I detested the nickname he insisted on calling me: *Tubby.*

Our visits to the property have kept the tradition of carving our initials into the old Madrone tree. The early childhood initials are far too high in the tree to find. The scars of more recent decades have been located. For many years, the nickname Tubby was much like the initials we carved in that tree. In spite of the growth, the scars remained.

Sometimes you have to grow up
before you appreciate how you grew up.

———

The House Across the Creek.

∞∞∞

Mary, niece RuthAnn, me, and Ron

∞ ∞ ∞

The Haunted House

"**I**t's the sound of an old house settling." My small framed mother stood with hands firmly placed on her hips as she adamantly informed us that the rumors were not true.

Our parents sold the shack and 40 acres across the creek and purchased a trio of houses a quarter mile south. We moved into the big house, an old two story home with seven bedrooms and one bath. No more tubs to be brought inside for bathing, no trips out back and no need for a Folgers can under our bed. I attended third grade the year we made the move. In spite of our mother's insistence that no spirits dwelled among us, the icy chill in the upstairs bedrooms hinted otherwise.

My brother Frank married shortly after our move to the big house. That left just Ron, Mary, me, Julie, and our niece, Karen, to grow up together. Karen, two years my elder, lived with us more often than not until mid-high school.

When the lawn wore blankets of frothy white, the girls doubled up in two of the five upstairs bedrooms. Those two rooms sandwiched a brick chimney, the only source of heat upstairs. My brother, Ron, cuddled under piles of blankets, his breath created a misty fog as he slept in his room.

Downstairs, my parents slept in one bedroom and the second bedroom became my father's library. It displayed his prized collection of Louis Lamour and Zane Gray books. It doubled as a quiet space for his 15-minute power nap before he left for his night shift job with the county where he made road signs. Both rooms were warm as long as the library's pot belly stove continued to be stoked with wood.

As spring approached, the upstairs temperatures rose. I moved into my own bedroom. I'd pull blankets over my head until I fell asleep. *See no evil, hear no evil.* My oldest sister, Ruth, slept in the back bedroom when she'd come to drop Karen off to live with us. Regardless of the season, that room never warmed. The eerie chill made the hair on my arms stand at attention. I also stayed out of my brother's room. If I had to enter his room alone, my eyes would be glued to the window seat, used to store blankets. When I completed the necessary task that took me there, I'd rush out so whatever unseen thing might be in the room couldn't grab me.

I'd made the mistake of watching a horror movie, *The Raven.* Dr. Craven needs a lock of dead man's hair for a potion. He and the Raven, a man turned into a bird, go to a dimly lit basement where everything is covered with an accumulation of dirt and dust. He slowly walks to a casket and stands silently for a second. The casket lid is stuck. He uses a knife to pry at the lid. It raises a little and drops quickly.

"Ouch!" The Raven squawks as his feathered fingers get pinched with the fall of the lid.

"I'm sorry." A second attempt is made to open the lid. It groans. Dirt and dust slide off. Then *Screech!* The rusty hinges echo in the dingy basement. The lid is now open and the two look into the casket at a gray-haired corpse. A curious, anticipating, expression crosses the Raven's face. Dr. Craven cautiously reaches into the casket.

"Forgive me Papa." his cold voice apologizes but his sneer seems anything but apologetic. He lifts a piece of long, gray hair. With his knife, he saws off the lock. His eyes grow wide and he stands frozen as he watches his father's hand come

23

to life. His father's corpse lifts his head; his hand grasps Dr. Craven's collar and pulls him within inches of his face. In a throaty growl, the corpse speaks. *"BeeeWarrre!"* His fingers loosen the grip. He falls back into the casket. Dr. Craven stumbles backward in a panic.

I knew the window box in my brother's bedroom contained extra blankets and nothing else, but my vivid imagination tried to convince me there might be more in that box. I've never watched another horror movie.

The flames of a small propane heater flickered as it warmed the dining room, the hub of our family activities. We listened to song requests on the radio while we worked on our homework. The large living room and parlor, with their bay windows and high ceilings got little use. The house had newspaper between the walls for insulation. Trying to heat the rooms with its small fireplace would be a waste of firewood. A long staircase led up to the only bathroom and our bedrooms — the same staircase that two previous owners swore they heard footsteps ascend and descend throughout the night.

A skid road that served as part of our driveway followed the hillside for miles each way. We walked that road to get to the tiny Wonder General Store and to visit our neighbors. The skid road was the old stagecoach route. The big house was once the stage stop hotel.

I was in eighth grade when the big house burned to the ground due to a flue fire. Historians estimated the house to be 125 years old when it went up in flames in 1964.

The second house, a much smaller two bedroom, became our home. We were back to using an outhouse until our father could install a septic and update the bathroom which, at the time, had a bathtub and running water, but no toilet. Dad turned the attic into two additional bedrooms which the girls all shared. This was home until I graduated high school. The third house on the property, a one-bedroom cabin with no bathroom, was sold some years later.

When asked today if I believe in ghosts, my response is: "No, not ghosts... but I do believe there are spirits among us." I think of the term *ghost* as a creature who haunts, depicted in horror movies. We saw no sign of that in the big house. I believe guardian angels protect us. I believe we have demons that terrorize the minds of many. We have another name for those demons now, we call them mental health issues.

I never feared living alone all the years I spent as a single woman. There were occasional nights after I turned off the light, that an eerie feeling loomed in my room. I'd pull my covers around me, cuddle into my pillow, and think, *If I turn to look, will someone... or something... be there?* I didn't look. Instead, I'd quietly whisper *Jesus Jesus Jesus.* It didn't take long to fall into a peaceful sleep. Waking later, the eeriness would be gone. My sister, Phyllis, once told me,

"I wish you would have looked!" It wasn't necessary. I didn't need, nor did I want, to know.

During the day I don't believe in ghosts. At night
I'm a little more open minded.

The Haunted House
(aka the Big House)

∞ ∞ ∞

Missed Opportunities

The PA system screeched. A pounding *thump thump thump* came next. "Testing, testing." *Screech, crackle, crackle, screech.*

"I want to announce the new cheerleaders for Lincoln Savage Junior High School." A deep authoritative voice boomed across the airway. A sense of dread came over me. I slumped in my chair, and pouted in silence. The winners' names were read. Mine not included.

Mary and I practiced cheers over and over at home. Our pep rally skirts twirled around us. We tossed our black and orange pom poms in the air. *Would I have won, IF I'd had the courage to try out? But... if I tried out and lost... I'd have been so embarrassed!* I resented my fears.

Mary and I were two years apart in age. My birthday is in October; hers is in December. With her birthday well into the school year, she started school at age seven rather than six like me. That put us only one year apart in grades. Then Mr. Rice held her back in her sixth grade year. From that point on, we were in the same classes. We lived 13 miles out of town, near the border of the Grants Pass School District and the Illinois Valley School District. After Mary and I completed our eighth grade year at Lincoln Savage Junior High, my siblings and I — actually it was mostly my siblings who spoke while I backed them — convinced our parents to let us transfer to Illinois Valley since our cousins lived in that district. I had hidden reasons for wanting to transfer. Lincoln Savage Junior High taught seventh through ninth grades. The

Illinois Valley district didn't have a junior high school. First through eighth grades attended the elementary school while ninth through twelfth grades were at the high school. That meant I would be in high school. *As a high schooler, life will be different.* I envisioned a miraculous change. Sports, dances, hanging with friends. I mentally, and physically, prepared for an adventurous year.

Ouch! I grit my teeth. *Yikes!* I grimaced with every hair plucked. When the numb, red skin returned to flesh color, I smiled. No more unibrow, which allowed my long black lashes and baby blue eyes to be the focus of my face. My hair shone a deeper shade of brunette, thanks to Miss Clairol. I admired my new look in the mirror. *I'm ready*, I thought. In the first week of high school student body elections were held. A classmate smiled as she looked in my direction.

"I nominate Esther Nelson for class treasurer." I gasped. She didn't warn me of her plan to nominate me. An involuntary muscle shot my hand high into the air, in a fierce wave.

"I decline!" I squeaked through air constricted vocal cords. The familiar blanket of disappointment wrapped itself around me. I slumped into it, pulled it over my head, and avoided eye contact with anyone. *I want to be class treasurer — but what if I lose?* My outer appearance had changed a bit, but the inner content remained the same.

> *I don't regret the things I've done. I regret the things I didn't do when I had the chance.*

Decades later I lay in my comfortable bed. I listened to the steady rhythmic breathing of my husband as he slumbered beside me. I have regular nights of insomnia. Enroute home from one of our trips, he'd suggested I write my life story for my children and grandchildren. As I lay beside him, I thought about my childhood days: growing up a country girl, swimming in Slate Creek, bike rides on the skid road that led to the Wonder store, target practice with a .22 rifle. I thought about the multi-colored hillside of autumn, soon covered with winter snow which meant time to pull out the snow sleds.

I recalled the warm summer nights when our parents allowed Ron, Mary, Julie, Karen and I to sleep outside, under a ceiling of stars. We watched for the satellite that could sometimes be spotted moving slowly across the sky. Two days before my 7th birthday, October 4, 1957, the USSR launched the first artificial satellite, *Sputnik*. In 1959, the Grants Pass Active Club sponsored the first annual Memorial Day event, featuring vendors, hydroplane races, and a carnival. They named it the *Boatnik*. It's an annual event to this date although when I ask, most people have no idea where the name originated.

On the lumpy mattress, we attempted to count the stars. In the rural darkness, unobscured by city lights, some stars sparkled like diamonds against the inky blackness, while others appeared faint, twinkling, as if they were playing a game with us — or shyly hiding. Losing track of our count, we huddled under our blankets until we fell asleep with the sweetness of the flowers, and the short, rhythmic chirping of a thousand crickets.

Much like my attempt to count the stars in my childhood, I lay awake in my bed, considering the vast stories throughout my life. Like the stars, some stories twinkle, some shine bright, others want to fade away or hide in the shadows, avoiding exposure. Each story played a role in my character, yet there are too many to include. I wondered if the brightest ones might find their way onto the pages, with no mention of the ones in hiding. Ironically, the stories hidden in the shadows are those that most need to be told. They best describe decades of my life; hiding, watching from the shadows, yearning, wishing I could shine as much as that brightest star!

∞ ∞ ∞

I relate to a quote I read in a Reader's Digest magazine:

"I heard opportunity knock on my door. By the time I removed the chain, turned back the bolt, and opened the door, it was gone."

Nothing is more expensive
than a missed opportunity.
H. Jackson Brown

∞ ∞ ∞

Chapter Three

Australia Bound

When we moved in together, I asked John to transfer me to a different KFC store location. Since he supervised multiple stores in the chain, he could do that. He also bought me an inexpensive wedding ring set. Seven months later, on June 7, 1971, we made it official. John and I stood at the courthouse, in front of a Justice of the Peace. Short, simple, traditional vows were said. We didn't publicize the wedding. John's father, and one of John's managers, served as witnesses.

Dad Stark worked at the nuclear plant in Centralia, an hour from our Seattle location. Mom Stark stayed in Fresno until John's younger sister graduated from high school. Concluding the vows, Dad treated us to dinner at Ivar's Seafood restaurant on the waterfront.

After we completed a fabulous seafood dinner, Dad drove back to Centralia and John and I went home to an empty house. We sold all our belongings, in anticipation of our move. Our clothes were packed, our king-size waterbed mattress drained, folded, and placed in the back window of our car. We slept on the carpeted floor with a blanket and pillow we'd kept out. At dawn we would toss those in the car and hit the road in our new Toyota Corolla, purchased just weeks earlier.

"I'm not so sure we should go into debt for that kind of money right now." That was the best I could do. He'd already made up his mind. I wanted to wave my arms to get his attention and firmly state, "we can't afford a car payment right now." Instead, I quietly sulked. I was raised in a family with a shoestring budget. I leaned toward careful discretion in spending. John still had monthly payments from his first marriage, plus child support. Regardless of my hesitation, we drove home a brand new 1971 Toyota Corolla that day. With its small contoured yellow body and black vinyl top, it looked like a bumble bee buzzing down the road. Total purchase price, $3,500.

When John got excited about something, he'd become hyper. He paced, his thoughts rushed out of his mouth, nearly babbling, as he verbalized his ideas. He reacted spontaneously, wanting to take action on those ideas right now. That's how he acted the day he sprang his newest idea on me. He said he'd been thinking about it for a long time.

"We have a whole new life ahead of us. Now's the time to do it!" His eyes glistened as he talked about a land down under. I quietly smiled, nodded, thinking *this idea will blow over soon... I hope.* The next morning we would be headed for new adventures. The Australian Consulate, with the idea of going to Australia, was placed first on the itinerary. *It's so far away. It's a risky decision. I can't believe we... he... could consider moving that far away.* I shuddered at the thoughts, eventually pushing them aside, letting his enthusiasm spark my interest. How can I not go?

As morning sunlight peeked through Seattle's gray, damp marine layer, we buzzed down the road. Two naive kids — ages 20 and 21 — setting off for San Francisco, hoping to realize John's dream. He talked, he laughed, his excitement stayed high as we drove south. He loved new things and I think he especially loved the unknown. In the midst of all the conversation, he made another suggestion.

"Let's do a little sightseeing before we go to San Francisco." I had no qualms about delaying a trip to Australia. Our sightseeing took us past San Francisco, to San Jose, where we drove by a brand-new building. A large sign read Bartel & Blaine A & W Restaurant, soon to open its doors for business. Another sign with large bold letters stood in the window. **NOW HIRING.** John pulled over and parked.

"Let's check it out."

"I'll wait out here. You go in." I leaned back, closed my eyes and slid down into the curve of the seat. The warmth of the California sun felt good... so good I entered dreamland within minutes. The car door opened, as did my eyes at the sound. An hour had passed. John climbed in the car, his eyes twinkling, a grin spread across his face.

"We need to find a place to live. They just hired me as Manager." I'm not sure how I hid my sigh of relief as it was strong enough to nearly collapse my chest. He never mentioned the subject of Australia again. Neither did I, and I hoped the subject had been buried for good. We found a quaint little one-bedroom, furnished duplex, separated by a garage from our landlord. It was hidden from the freeway by a row of tall trees. On the other side of the freeway was the San Jose airport. As the planes came in for landing, we could almost see the outline of passengers in the windows of the low flying crafts.

Throughout our marriage, John's imagination instigated a lot of our adventures. I admired his take-charge personality. It fueled my courage to follow him into areas I'd never have gone on my own. It was easy to follow in his shadow. Where his confidence came from, I'm not sure. He talked little of his childhood days and when he did, the conversations hinted at discontentment. He left home at age 17 and joined the Navy.

Ten months later, the Navy discharged him. He didn't belong in an environment where he had to take orders from others, is what John told me.

That trait carried into his work history. He had leadership qualities and never worked well under others. At every move we made, his management skills landed him a job within a few days.

As I reminisce of the Australia plan, I chuckle. There were a few details we overlooked at the time. Neither of us had passports. I'm sure we didn't have funds for plane tickets either. And, what about that new car we just purchased? What we did have was a dream.

A single dream can be more powerful
than a thousand realities.

∞ ∞ ∞

Opposites

Our personalities were polar opposites. Like the north and south poles of two magnets, our differences attracted us to one another. I longed to have the confidence and courage to speak my mind like John did.

I have no recollection of the first time John or I said the words, "I love you." I don't deny I felt an attraction from the moment we met, when my gaze flashed to his hand to check for a ring. I thought I'd promptly dismissed any notion, but perhaps I'd merely buried it deep within. Maybe that's why I responded the way I did when he unexpectedly appeared at my doorstep. As we spent more time together, our connection grew. I'd fall asleep with my head nestled on his shoulder or chest. We cuddled into a spoon position, our bodies entwined like two pieces of a puzzle. Throughout the night we moved in tandem, our bodies adjusting to maintain the same intimate position.

And though I don't recall our first "I love you," I do know that eventually it was something we expressed on a daily basis. He could make me laugh... and cry... at the drop of a dime. John liked living on the edge whereas I nearly trembled at any thought of stepping outside of my safe zone. Our lives together were filled with changes, new places, new challenges, all different from the stable secure life in which I'd been raised.

My parents' generation didn't publicly exhibit affection, either physical or verbal. I didn't hear the words "I love you" as a child. I never felt unloved, it just wasn't something my parents said. Since I didn't hear the words, I didn't know how to say them either. My sister, Phyllis, wrote letters home frequently. She signed them with "I love you" at the end. I admired her for doing that. It was something I noticed in every letter. I struggled to vocalize my feelings even as an adult. I had good intentions to change that, with each phone call home. *End the call with "I love you,"* I'd tell myself.

I squirmed as I talked with my mother on the phone. If it was cordless, I would have been nervously pacing as well. I wanted to say "I love you" at the end of the call. I didn't do it that day. The next phone call, before I hung up the receiver of my blue princess telephone, I blurted, "I love you, Mom," …then *CLICK.* I hung up before she could respond. I didn't want to put her on the spot, to respond in kind, and how would I feel if she didn't reciprocate? Time went by before the next phone call but I was determined I would say it again.

"I love you, Mom." This time I paused — and I heard her response.

"Me too," she said. I placed the receiver in the cradle, my eyes wet. The ice had been broken. *Hopefully it will be easier from this point forward.* I dabbed the tears from my cheeks. I sat in my chair, my thoughts traveling back in time… to my high school graduation day.

Our similarities bring us to common ground;
Our differences allow us to be fascinated by each other.

My parents
Verdie (Peach) and Les Nelson

∞∞∞

ESTHER STARK

It was 1968

I graduated high school in 1968. It was an era of the Vietnam war and hippies. As guys graduated and turned 18, they were drafted into the army. Many married their high school sweethearts before being shipped out. Hippies infiltrated the small quaint town of Cave Junction, and the surrounding area. They formed a commune in Takilma. It was common to see men or women, holey jeans or long skirts, logging boots and long tangled hair, sitting beside the road, thumbs out, hoping for a ride. With their mantra, *Make Love, Not War*, they also brought free love and hallucinogenic drugs to town. My little high school town, consisting of one main street and no signal lights, soon acquired a reputation as a hippie town.

My sister, Mary, dropped out of high school and eloped to Reno, marrying one of our classmates. I was the first to graduate high school with eight elder siblings so my parents celebrated. Crepe paper streamers, tied to our car's antenna, whipped wildly in the wind. Signs that read *Congratulations Esther* were taped to the car doors. I slid low in the back seat. I kept my face away from the window.

"You can drop me at the curb." When we arrived at the school, I quickly exited the car and entered the building. The room buzzed with chatter as 56 excited classmates slipped into their robes. They helped each other place the hat and tassel at the precise angle. The girls' big hairdos, ratted and sprayed with Aqua Net, required bobby pins to secure the hats.

"Are you ready?" asked a teacher, poking her head in the doorway. The room fell silent. The faint sound of music could be heard in the distance, the cue for the junior class to start the processional. They carried arches covered with red and white roses that matched our robes. Guys wore red, gals wore white, our school colors. My skin tingled with excitement as I lined up with my good friend and walking partner, Gary Shean.

"We did it!" I whispered to Gary as I placed my arm through his.

"Yes, we did!" Amidst the bustle of classmates, I'd temporarily forgotten about the decorated car. It quickly came back to me as Gary and I reached the gymnasium doorway. I caught a glimpse of my father who stood at the back of the room. He held a large sign high above his head. The bold black letters read, *Esther Nelson, Our Queen.* My stomach lurched. I felt the blood drain from my face.

My father caught my eye as we walked in. I forced an awkward smile. My clench tightened on Gary's arm. He glanced at me. His eyes followed my horrified gaze toward my father. Spotting the sign, Gary patted my hand that held the death grip on his arm. He smiled, and gave me a wink of reassurance as if to say, "It's ok." His silent understanding helped me to relax. I smiled again and gave a nod of recognition to my father. I avoided eye contact with anyone else as we marched to the music towards the stage.

It's only embarrassing if you care what people think.

My father had no idea, ever, how those signs affected me that night. I realized he stepped far beyond the barrier of his comfort zone, expressing his love in the way he did. I will never forget June 6, 1968. Not because presidential candidate Bobby Kennedy died that day from an assassin's bullet. Not because I graduated from high school on that date. There is another reason I can never forget that date. I'll always remember June 6, 1968 because my father reached out, took me in his arms with tears in his eyes, and for the first time ever... I heard him whisper in my ear,

"I love you, sweetheart!"

I cried.

No one is afraid of saying "I Love You." They are afraid of the response.

Me at graduation - June 6, 1968

———

If I ever have children, they will hear the words "I love you" on a regular basis. I made that vow to myself. A vow I kept. My youngest son, Duane, ran toward me as he played. I reached out and grabbed my little preschooler. I pulled him close to me. With childlike excitement in my voice, I asked,

"Do you want to know a secret?"

"Yeah!" his eyes widened with expectation. What little boy doesn't want to know a secret?

"I love you." I whispered in his ear. He pulled back from me. His boyish grin faded and his giggles stopped. His brows scrunched with disappointment as he looked me in the eyes.

"That's not a secret!"

"What? Have you been telling people?" I asked, a teasing reprimand in my voice.

"No! Everybody knows that, cause you're my mom!"

A phone call with any one of my four sons seldom ends without an "I love you" before we disconnect.

Remember to say, "I love you" daily.

∞∞∞

Chapter Four

Roads Less Traveled

"You've seen so many places and done so many things, Esther. I envy you." My niece, Karen, spoke softly. Diagnosed with terminal cancer in her sixties, she confided in me of the desires she had as a young mother. She raised her family in the same home in which I grew up. The same home in which she too spent many years when her mother would drop her off for my parents to care for. She and her husband purchased my parents' house after Mom and Dad retired.

"I had a baby at age 16, married at a young age, and raised five children. I've never left my hometown, never traveled, never done anything exciting. You've lived all over the country and have done so much in life," she told me.

I always suspected people may be quietly judging me and John for all the moves we made, thinking it was a sign of instability, immaturity, or a lack of common sense. But after listening to Karen's story, I saw my life differently.

My sisters and I had a *Sister's Bash* weekend every four or five years. Just months before Karen passed, we held our sister weekend at my home and we invited Karen. We printed a certificate and signed it, unofficially adopting her as one of our sisters. After all, she grew up in our home more like a sister than a niece. It was an emotional moment for all of us.

The plan to move from the greater Seattle area to Australia was only the beginning of our impulsive moves. John's discontentment with a job, or life circumstances, often being the catalyst which propelled us from town to town, job to job. Sometimes reluctant, but always conceding, I was willing to be co-pilot on each journey. Our resumes became a multitude of experiences.

Now, at an older age, I count my blessings of the adventures I've experienced; the places I've seen, and lived. If not for John's wild ideas and ambitions, I may have had a similar story as Karen.

Relocations took us to six states, saw the births of our four sons, prompted the start, as well as the end, of several of our own businesses, and led us on a roller coaster ride of electrifying ups and tumultuous soul searching downs. If something wasn't going quite right for us, we'd decide a new place, a new job, would make things better. We would decide on a location, pack up the car, and hit the road. For the first eight years of our marriage, we lived in 21 different homes. Much like my erroneous thinking that attending high school would change my personality — our moves had similar results.

———

Though John always landed a job in short order, I took time to get settled. I dreaded the job search and interviews. Marketing my job qualities was not easy for me to do.

"You know you can do anything you want, if you put your mind to it." John had more faith in my abilities than I did. After we dismissed the idea of Australia, John worked for Bartel & Blaine in San Jose for a year when they offered him a promotion as manager of a new A&W Restaurant on the beaches of Pacifica, California, just south of San Francisco. I had been hired as a manager at Manning's Cafeteria in San Jose. Once we settled in San Jose, John wanted a baby. I quit taking my pills and was soon pregnant. When we relocated to Pacifica, I didn't look for work.

The new A&W building was unique in its design. Built on the beach, partially on stilts, allowed the incoming tide to flow under the deck. The irresistible environment of the salty ocean breeze, rolling waves, and seagulls that perched nearby to beg for a french fry, made this a popular venue for fast food junkies and beachcombers. After two months on the job, the owners were hinting to John about a possible promotion to general manager.

"Wish me luck! The owners want to meet with me this morning." John had a hopeful grin on his face. He gave me a hug before sprinting out the door. An hour later the door crashed open, shaking the walls of our sparsely furnished one-bedroom apartment. His grin was gone, replaced by a firmly clenched jaw. His eyes were dark with rage. There had been an unexplainable error on a recent inventory. John got the blame. They fired him.

"I'm done with food service," he fumed.

Within days our Toyota bumble bee headed north to Grants Pass, Oregon. My parents offered to let us stay with them until the baby's arrival, due in one month.

————

I read a news article 48 years later titled:

"Newly Remodeled Taco Bell on the Coast Serves Alcohol."

I had no interest in an article about Taco Bell's ability to serve alcohol. It was the photograph that caught my eye. The article stated:

"The Taco Bell, located in Pacifica, California was originally owned by Bartel & Blaine and was built in the early 1970's."

That night I searched for the scrapbook which, at one time, held a sketch I'd drawn of the A&W building. I'd sometimes walk to John's place of work for lunch. One day I took a sketch book, sat in the warmth of the California sun and sketched the building. I didn't find the drawing that night. What I did find was a newspaper article dated March 29, 1972.

"The new A&W on the beach is owned by the parent company Bartel & Blaine. The manager is John Stark who recently moved to Pacifica after a year with the company in the San Jose area."

That 1972 article had a photograph of John cutting the ribbon during the grand opening. I placed my hand on the faded photograph in the news article as if it would take me back in time. It did, for a few moments.

*When you come to a fork in the path, be adventurous,
take the Road Less Traveled.*

Now a Taco Bell, this building was built as an A&W
Rootbeer establishment, opening in March 1972.

∞ ∞ ∞

A Baby and A Business

"Esther, wake up. Look!" I quickly sat up to see what warranted my attention. John slowed the car, allowing a doe and her fawn to cross the road. I groaned. John spent his childhood days in Fresno, California, a city boy. I spent my childhood as a country girl.

"Cool." *That's what he woke me for?* I tried to show some enthusiasm but I'd have preferred not to be awakened to see a deer. Those were animals that grazed on our lawn, and jumped the garden fences to eat my father's vegetables. On occasion, the grunts and groans of a bear meandering down our long driveway during the night could be heard. I had nightmares about bears for years, always afraid of those big black fur balls. "They're more afraid of you than you are of them" people often say. Not true. I know I'm more afraid of them. There had been several cougar sightings over the years. On those days, we were not allowed to play outside after dark. I was accustomed to having wildlife in our yard.

Within a week of arriving in Oregon, John went to work as a choker setter for a logging company in Happy Camp, where my brother-in-law worked, just over the Oregon/California border. Logging was a family business before my birth. My grandfather once owned a sawmill and my father owned a small logging company. Many of my relatives were loggers. Timber was Oregon's number one industry for decades — until environmental arguments over old-growth forest and the threatened northern spotted owl halted logging projects and shut down many lumber mills.

John, the city boy, was inexperienced with the timber industry, which led him to be extremely cautious. He knew there were dangers involved with the work. He had an uncle who was killed in a logging accident. I remember John's mother crying when we told her he took a job in the woods.

"If you hear rumbling, get the hell out of there and hide behind a log. It may be a log that broke free and is rolling down the hillside," his co-workers warned him. One day John heeded their warning when a loud *CRACK!* rang through the air, followed by a long rumble, much like the snapping of a cable, a log on the loose. Since John worked downhill from the trucks being loaded, he took instant action, diving behind a huge log for protection. The rumble stopped. Lightning and thunder gave the loggers a good laugh, at John's expense. He chuckled as he told me the story although I detected a mixture of animosity that he'd been the butt of a little redneck fun.

John stayed in my brother-in-law's 16-foot travel trailer at the logging camp during the week, and came back to my parents' place on the weekends. At five o'clock on the morning of June 15, 1972, my mother left a message for John.

"Meet us at the hospital. Esther is in labor." I curled into a fetal position, holding my breath, trying to ease the pain. *Breathe Esther.* I reminded myself. *But it hurts to breathe. The baby must be ready to come right now!* I tried to hold back my tears. My tiny 5'2" mother held onto me as I wobbled my way to the car. I laid across the back seat where a sense of panic struck. We are 13 miles from town. *Correna was born in my mother's car right here in this very driveway*, I recalled.

My brother, George and his wife Linda, lived in a small trailer on my parents' property in 1965, while I was in high school. Linda waited too long. When she decided to go to the hospital, they had only reached the end of the long driveway when Linda cried out that the baby was coming. My mother turned the car around and drove back to the house. Linda gave birth to Correna in the back seat. I didn't want that same experience. I prayed we'd make it to the hospital.

"You're dilated to about two. It will be a while." My doctor's calm voice annoyed me. *He must be wrong!*

"That's all?" I squeaked. I resented his words — as if this was all his fault.

"I need to go out of town for the day. I'll check on you when I get back this evening. If need be, I'll break your water then. That will prompt the baby's birth." He left the room. I groaned, and wondered, *Why can't he break the water now?* I hoped he was wrong. *There are plenty of staff members who can help with the birth, if the baby arrives before he gets back.* I prayed, I panted, I groaned, I pushed, I cried, for another 15 hours. John sat in a chair near my head. He tried to encourage me. In my short moments of silence, he would fall asleep, only to be awakened by another lengthy moan from me. Determined to have my baby by natural birth, I refused any medication. The baby stayed patient, waiting for the doctor to return around nine o'clock that night.

"Let's take a look," he said. He asked the nurse to prepare me for delivery and broke my water. Lawrence (soon nicknamed Larry) James Stark — named for both, his father, John Lawrence, and his grandpa, Lawrence Richard — arrived within the hour, healthy and strong.

"It's a little towhead boy!" the doctor exclaimed. I was elated. A boy is what I wanted. I couldn't help feeling a little offended by what the doctor said though — I didn't know the meaning of towhead, but it didn't sound complimentary. My mother soothed my feathers by informing me a towhead just meant he had a head full of blond hair. Baby Lawrence and I went home from the hospital two days later, on June 17, 1972, Father's Day.

∞∞∞

Me and John - May 1972

∞∞∞

Me with Larry

June 17, 1972

I pulled the collar of my sweater up around my neck as the brisk wind slapped my long hair against my cheeks, stinging my face. The ocean air reeked of salty, sour seaweed. When we accepted the offer to lease Barney's Burger Joint in Lincoln City, on the Oregon coast, I'd envisioned warm sandy beaches.

I'm not sure why. I grew up in Grants Pass, a two hours drive to Brookings, on Oregon's coast. My father loved fishing there. The Oregon coast is a beautiful showcase for the magnificent rugged cliffs. It has rocky beaches scattered with tide pools, roads that wind through tall Redwood, Fir and Pine trees, and powerful waves that crash over the sea walls and against the jetties. April through June the Pacific Rhododendron and Azaleas broadcast a brilliant show of colors along the roadside. It is not known for having warm weather. Lincoln City is also known for its kite festivals. Why would I be surprised at the weather that greeted us that day?

Bill Blake, a friend of my father's, was in the process of purchasing the currently closed Barneys Burger Joint. When my father mentioned John's experience with food service, Bill made John an offer — a short-term lease, lasting the remainder of the summer season. The business would close when Labor Day brought an end to the tourist season. A lease renewal would be an option for the beginning of the next year's season. The purchase by Blake fell through in the end and a renewal was no longer on the horizon but we were allowed to finish the summer season. Being a short term lease, John was anxious to get started. Larry was two-weeks-old when we made the move to Lincoln City. We worked quickly, and opened Barneys in time for the 4th of July weekend. The small hamburger stand had a walk-up window and outside patio seating. No inside seating.

Finding a place to live became a challenge with the tourist season in full swing. We borrowed the 16-foot camp trailer where John stayed while logging and it served as temporary sleeping quarters. The campground, where we parked, provided restrooms and showers. It was a busy summer running Barneys, which became a popular fast-food spot. Customers from the neighboring go-kart track flocked to the window to order the sizzling hot, 19-cent hamburgers. At dinner time it wasn't unusual for a customer to order 10 or 20 hamburgers to take home for families. John and I worked well together. Since he trained me in my first job, I'd learned the quality of work he expected and I performed it well.

Knowing the lease was short lived, John watched for other opportunities. He had a taste of his own business and was determined to fulfill that goal again. The day we closed the doors of Barney's, he signed the lease on a Texaco gas station in town.

"You know that's not something I can help with." I had no interest in working at a gas station. A part of me was annoyed he'd choose such a business and another part of me entertained the enjoyment of being a stay-at-home-mom with my infant son.

"I know. I'm going to get your dad to come up here." John's confidence amazed me. What made him so sure he could talk my father into moving to Lincoln City?

"Good luck with that idea!" I rolled my eyes and gave a sarcastic laugh. He would not only have to talk my father into it but my mother as well.

The tourist season ended, and we found a quaint, picturesque cottage perched high on a hillside. The front picture window framed a spectacular view of the Pacific Ocean. I couldn't believe we were able to rent this gem for $90 per month. We paid twice that amount for a small apartment in California, with no view.

John called my father and made a proposal. He formed an instant bond with my father when they first met. They didn't have much in common except they were both quick to speak their minds. John, always blunt, to the point, with no tact. Dad was always gruff and opinionated. Maybe it was a language they both understood.

"I'll talk to Peach," my dad said.

"You mean he's actually going to consider it?" I was shocked. John shrugged and nodded.

"That's what he said."

Dad retired the year I graduated high school. He'd bought a carnival ride and they traveled with the carnival several summers before he sold the ride. That's how he met Bill Blake. Bill owned a traveling carnival. I knew my father loved the Oregon coast, but to leave his home and move to the coast? I hoped John wouldn't be too disappointed when they turned down the offer. Several days later, to my surprise, John received a call. My parents accepted. They sold their home to my niece, Karen, and her husband. The apartment they found in Lincoln City had an opening for an assistant manager, a position they filled. Better yet, it was one block from us — a perfect location where my father could sit near his living room window and watch the ocean.

John and Dad pumped gasoline at 35 cents a gallon. They listened to constant customer complaints, "It's only 25 cents inland. How come it's so expensive on the coast?" A selection of tires filled a large rack; fan belts and various hoses hung on the garage walls. Shelves were stocked with common auto parts. John made minor engine repairs and they both changed oil and pumped gas. The station seemed to give my father a sense of pride, to be working successfully alongside John. If you listened to their banter, you'd think they were at each other's throats. I'd bristle at the thought of them arguing sometimes, only to find neither was offended at the other's harsh words. It was just their way of communicating, and they did it well. I'd always been a person who avoided confrontations, if at all possible. When classmates gathered around to watch a fight at school, I always went the other way, appalled at the scene.

John worked long hours, weekends, and holidays with Dad's assistance. On Christmas morning, a long line of cars required a deputy to direct traffic. We were the only gas station open within a 120-mile stretch. Cars were backed up waiting to get fuel. On that same Christmas morning, Larry, now six months old, cut his two bottom front teeth. After spending a fussy night, he cuddled with me as he nursed. I shrieked and pulled him away from me. His tiny jaws clenched tight. Repeat occurrences of biting led to a quick weaning process.

One afternoon John walked in the house unexpectedly, fire shooting from his eyes. He slammed the letter he'd been carrying onto the kitchen table.

"There's no way in hell they can do that!" He pointed at the letter. I had no idea what the letter said, or who it was from. I stepped back, wanting to keep my distance. The violent tone in his voice frightened me. I'd never seen him this angry. I waited for him to explain.

The government planned to ration gasoline. The letter indicated our allotment would be based on the previous year's sales. John was open twice the hours than the last person who ran that station. Anxious for his lease to end, the former proprietor closed early, opened later, and closed on holidays. Despite John's appeals, our gasoline allotment came in at half the amount of fuel we typically pumped. Not wanting to run out and have the pumps closed until a new shipment of fuel was received, he limited his pumping hours. He kept the garage open all day, selling tires and parts, doing repairs and oil changes.

John's smile disappeared; his mood darkened. It was as if a cloud followed him around. He watched, not knowing what else to do, as his dream slowly crumbled. He brought home a six pack of beer each night. One evening the hospital called. John was in a head-on collision. "He's ok. He's being treated for minor injuries." Both vehicles were totaled, both drivers were under the influence. I have no clue why the officer didn't cite either of them. Maybe he thought they'd paid the consequences with their injuries. John had two broken wrists and deep lacerations on his face. A scar on his upper lip and a two-inch scar across his left cheek became lifetime reminders of the incident. The other driver had minor injuries. Within a few days John was back to work with Dad, casts on both arms as he pumped gasoline. As business dropped and income dwindled, John's depression worsened. He wouldn't talk about it. I didn't pressure him. And I kept silent about another situation that concerned me. John had enough stress; he didn't need something else to worry about.

Larry lay cuddled on my chest as I rocked back and forth. My mother sat close by, and we visited with not much more than a whisper to keep from waking the baby. We jumped as the blaring *WHOOP WHOOP* of a siren rang through the air. Larry's head bolted up, his eyes wide with fright. He began to wail. My mother went to the window, the sirens stopped.

"It looks like they stopped in front of your house, Esther." Running to the window, I saw an ambulance and police car parked in front of our cottage, the paramedics running up the long steps to our house. I thrust Larry into my mother's arms and ran out the door.

Broken lamps, the coffee table and end tables were strewn across the front lawn. Jagged pieces of glass were scattered everywhere, evidence the furniture came through the large picture window. Officers tried to secure John's flinging arms, ignoring his shouts of profanity. After restraining, they placed him in the ambulance.

"We'll transport him to the hospital in Salem," the paramedic told me. *Why not the hospital here in town?* I wondered. I didn't ask. I never questioned authority, or anyone for that matter. I arranged for mom to keep Larry, and I drove to Salem, an hour away. I waited for the doctors. John hadn't appeared injured, their reason for transporting him to the hospital was troubling. *And why to Salem,* I wondered. I was shocked when they told me he suffered a mental breakdown. After I answered all their questions, and gave them my explanation of his recent stress, they explained.

"Think of a match being tossed into a puddle of gasoline. It explodes. Alcohol added to stress can do the same. It can set off a psychotic episode. That seems to be what happened to John."

My dad ran the station while they kept John under observation for a week. When he was ready to be released, I drove over to pick him up. He climbed in the car. No eye contact. I was sure he was feeling embarrassed.

"How are you doing?" I cautiously asked him.

"I'm fine!" The sharpness in his voice told me not to question any further and we rode the hour home in silence. No antidepressants or other medication had been prescribed – at least not to my knowledge. If so, John never filled a prescription. We didn't talk openly about our problems so his response wasn't unusual. We swept it under the carpet, out of sight, out of mind.

A dying business and an uncomfortable situation were the signal to John that it was time to move on. John's father suggested registering with the Labor Union in the Tri-Cities. John would have a good chance of being called out on the Hanford Nuclear Plant where his dad worked. John registered. He made weekly trips to check in with the union. Larry and I often rode with him. We enjoyed our stops along the Columbia River where we searched for agates in the gravel piles and along the shore. With another move in the works, it was time to tell John. I wouldn't be able to keep it secret much longer.

"I stopped nursing Larry after Christmas. I haven't started my period. I'm sure I'm pregnant." I blurted it out, not sure how he'd respond. His eyes lit up. I was afraid it would give him one more thing to worry about. Instead, he was excited.

"Are you sure?"

"I haven't been to the doctor because we've had so much going on. I wanted to wait until I was sure. Now, I am."

The future belongs to those who believe in the beauty of their dreams."- Eleanor Roosevelt

∞ ∞ ∞

John pushes a disabled vehicle
at the Texaco station.

∞ ∞ ∞

Things My Sister Told Me

There was a light tap on the door. An elderly, balding male in scrubs entered. His eyes stayed glued to the chart in his hand while his head shook back and forth. He made an inaudible grumble, then a *tsk tsk* sound of disapproval. I sat timidly at the edge of the exam table. I kept the thin white, front opening gown pulled tight around me. He raised his head and with the flip of his hand gestured toward the exam table.

"Lay back on the table. I'll get some measurements." His voice was gruff. He pulled the gown open, exposing my belly. I flinched as he placed the icy cold tape-measure over my bulge, the size of a small watermelon.

"If you haven't been to a doctor yet, what makes you think you're pregnant?" His voice had an arctic chill to it. Feeling humiliated and belittled, I clenched my jaw, trying to hold back the tears. I pulled the flimsy gown around me and hopped off the table. I didn't look at him. I couldn't. I just stood there, not answering. He grumbled under his breath and walked out the door.

I found another doctor who listened intently as I explained the circumstances: no birth control taken while nursing; weaning process late December through January; no health insurance; waited until we moved to see a doctor. Now we are into July, and I've felt movement for some time. He responded with compassion and understanding. Ultrasounds weren't utilized during my child bearing days unless a medical issue indicated a concern.

"It's hard to tell without menstrual dates to calculate. You could have conceived at any point after you quit nursing, or even while you nursed for that matter. The baby feels small. I'd estimate a due date to be early October. We'll know more as time gets closer."

In mid-September I saw the doctor again.

"The baby's heartbeat is strong. Everything appears normal. It's still hard to tell about a date. Don't be too disappointed if you don't deliver until the middle of October."

John and I were renting a two-bedroom duplex about a mile from his parents. John's sister, Nancy, gave birth to a baby boy on September 20th. They made the trip to southern California to meet their new grandson.

"We should be back by your due date, Esther," they said. I arranged to pick up their mail and place it in the house. It gave me some exercise, and Larry loved the stroller ride. On the 25th of September, I put Larry in the stroller and set out for our daily walk. I hoped the walk would relieve the tight muscles in my back. I took the usual route, stopping every so often to bend and stretch. I gathered the mail and placed it on the table. The walk exhausted me and I still needed to walk the mile back home. I took Larry from the stroller and let him play while I slunk into Dad Stark's recliner to relax. The return trip was much the same; stretching, bending, trying to work the pinched feeling from my back. I explained the situation to John when he returned from work. He massaged my low back. The relief lasted a short time.

"If I didn't know better, I'd think I was starting labor." I told John as we climbed into bed that night. He offered to take me to the hospital but I'd just seen the doctor a few days before. "It's probably just the position the baby is in that makes me so uncomfortable. It's not really painful, just pinching." John sat next to me in bed, reading a book. As the evening worn on the pinch got stronger and the groans more frequent.

"I'm calling the doctor!" he said.

"Go to the hospital. I'll meet you there. It's probably false labor but we don't want to take any chances," the doctor told John.

Since John's parents were still out of town, John called a family friend Merle, asking her to stay with Larry while we made the trip to the hospital. Kadlec Hospital was only a mile from our duplex.

"I'll bring Elaine right over. She can spend the night."

My hands were shaking as I slipped into my maternity blue jeans and a shirt, then curled up on the bed. It was just past midnight. It didn't take long for Merle and her teenage daughter to arrive. John came into the bedroom to get me.

"Merle is here. We better go." His voice sounded a little nervous. I swung my legs over the side of the bed. John came around to help me. When I tried to stand, my legs wobbled like Jell-O and I fell back to the bed. John scooped me up and carried me through the hallway. Merle held the front door open for us. At the door, my back arched involuntarily. A sharp, vice-grip pain squeezed my waist. My water broke, drenching my blue jeans. I gasped. Through clenched teeth, I managed,

"You better hurry! I can feel the baby's head, and it's coming right now!"

"I'm going with you to keep John calm!" Merle shouted over my groan. John laid me across the front seat and Merle climbed in the back. He drove fast, in silence, but I could hear Merle as she

61

leaned over me from the back seat,

"What should I do? What should I do?" she shrieked.

"Help me get my pants off!" The pain heaved my back into another arch. I struggled to get the elastic waistband below my belly. I could tell the baby's arrival was being stopped by a pair of blue jeans. The car jolted to a stop. My body no longer wrenched; my semi-conscious mind tried to focus. A red sign appeared blurry as I peered out the window. *Emergency.*

I heard the driver's door open, muddled voices in the distance, then Merle's voice, half sobs, half laughter.

"It's a boy!" She yelled.

Our baby was full term with long dark hair and long fingernails — born right at nine months after I weaned Larry.

My mother never discussed personal things with us girls as we grew up. After the birth of my first son, my sister, Margie told me, "You won't have your period when you're nursing so you can't get pregnant." In the midst of my second pregnancy, I often wondered why I was so naive as to take birth control advice from Margie, who had seven children of her own — but on this very night, as I gazed at the face of my newborn, I was glad I did!

> *Your son will hold your hand for a little while,*
> *but your heart for a lifetime.*

∞ ∞ ∞

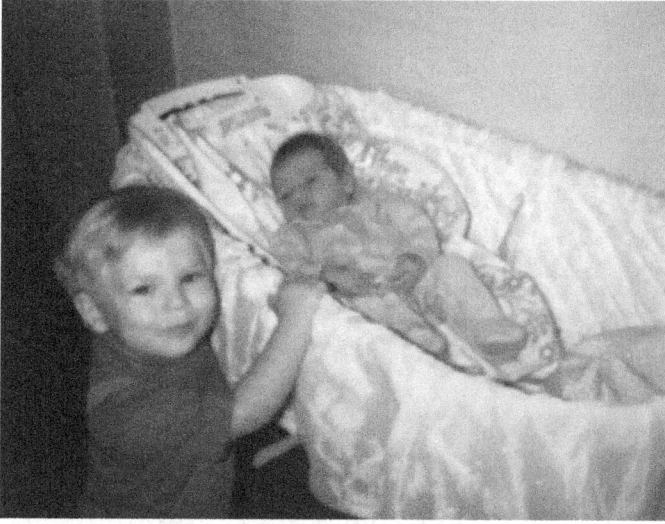

Larry with baby Stephen.

Chapter Five

The Devil's Advocate

John loved to debate... any subject. If I offered any kind of opinion, he would oppose — wanting me to defend my opinion. I couldn't do that. I didn't know how to do that. I didn't have the grit needed to stand my ground. If he said I was wrong, then I'd drop the subject, or I'd get extremely defensive. He relished in playing the devil's advocate, and I hated it.

After John died in 1992, Jim Harding, President of the Oregon Paralyzed Veterans of America, reflected on his experience with John in an article published in its newsletter (John served as Secretary on OPVA's Board of Directors):

"John touched my life in ways, until now, I hadn't realized. John was a wise counsel to me as Vice President, then President, of OPVA. At board meetings he was my antithesis on many issues, causing me to research issues closely, and develop sound reasons for the direction I wanted to take the organization. On several occasions I would call him after a board meeting wondering what was the license number of the truck that just ran over me. He would say, "I agree completely with your views on those issues, I just wanted you to examine them in more detail."

That was the same process John used on me. When I'd voice a rare opinion, he'd question me. I'd try to dismiss the subject but he'd continue nit-picking, pushing every button, until the threads holding my patience at bay wore thin, and snapped. At that point, every frustration, every disagreement we'd had, every annoyance I'd swept under the carpet and ignored, came out with a vengeance. Like a roaring lioness, I verbally attacked. During one such encounter, John interrupted me.

"If you're going to yell, close the window so the neighbors don't have to hear." He seemed to think that would soothe my anger. Instead, I flounced to the window, slammed it shut, and continued.

"I never know what you're thinking unless I make you mad," he told me one day. Neither of us communicated well but the technique he used to get me to spill my guts wasn't the cure. When I became that angry, I'm sure I said things I didn't mean... although in the heat of the argument, I thought I did. Each incident seemed to plunge a wedge between us, making it even harder for me to express an opinion the next time.

John despised the labor union job at the Hanford Nuclear Plant but he showed up for work day after day, on time. For him, logic meant to make a profit by the end of the month. He couldn't understand the cost-plus union job.

"I can't even carry a piece of lumber to someone who needs it," he gnarled as he popped open a can of beer. "A carpenter has to do that!"

We seldom socialized with friends; actually we seldom made friends. We visited his parents who lived close by; we enjoyed going out to the desert where we spent afternoons skeet shooting; and he fished and hunted birds. I went duck hunting with him one bone-chilling morning. The too-early morning hour and sitting behind a duck blind freezing my tush, was not an enjoyable sport for me. Thereafter, duck and pheasant hunting was something he did alone, or occasionally with his dad.

As he grew more and more frustrated with the union job, he drank more, creating tension between us. It didn't take much to anger him. I grew weary of keeping my guard up with everything I said. As the alcohol increased, our arguments increased. When I'd hear the *POP*, then sizzle of an opened beer can, a wall went up between us. I'd stay in another room as much as possible — away from an inevitable blow up. I resented the stale smell of empty beer cans and the stench of overflowing ashtrays as I straightened up around his chair each morning. One evening World War III broke out between us. I jerked my hand loose from his grip on my wrist.

"I'm sick of arguing every night!" Tears flooded my eyes as I screamed the words at him.

"Then leave!" he spat, flinging his pointed finger toward the front door. I retreated to the bedroom. The closed door muffled the familiar thud of his fist hitting the wall. Windows rattled as he slammed the front door. Tires squealed. Two-year-old Larry, Stephen, not quite one, and I caught a plane to Oregon the next day. John called often wanting to reconcile.

"Why can't you just come home so we can work things out?" His anger confirmed my reason for being in Oregon. He called a second time, obviously under the influence. This call concerned me. John's parents lived not far from our duplex in Richland, Washington. I dialed Dad Stark. I told him of my concern and asked him to check on John. He did and returned my call several hours later.

"I got him calmed down." Dad paused. "He was drunk and busted up all the furniture. He had pieces of it scattered all over the yard."

"He can get so angry and violent when he's drinking," I confessed to Dad.

John quit the union job and returned to Seattle shortly after that incident — back to where we first met — back to the KFC Corporation, as District Manager for his former employer — back to the work he excelled at — where his skills were valued. He called often. He missed the boys. I wanted John to be near his sons but I wasn't sure I wanted to reconcile at this point. I remembered how devastated he was at losing his son, Mark, after he and his first wife divorced. She moved to southern California and remarried. John saw Mark when Mark was one, before they moved to New York. Though he paid his child support monthly, he never saw Mark again. Due to the prohibitive cost of air travel in that era, flying a toddler back and forth across the country for visitation was not feasible.

After several months in Oregon, I decided to move to the Seattle area, where John would be able to visit the boys. I rented a basement bedroom at my sister, Margie's place. She also agreed to provide daycare for the boys, while I managed a bustling cafeteria in the Tacoma Mall. A month later, John and I took the first steps towards reconciliation. We were determined to overcome our struggles and rebuild our relationship. It wasn't easy. Regardless, John and I navigated the minefield of past hurts, learned to forgive, and, like Dorothy in the *Wizard of Oz,* we followed the yellow brick road to places unknown to us.

And suddenly you just know...
it's time to start something new
and trust the magic of beginnings.

∞∞∞

Following the Yellow Brick Road

O ver the next eight years, the yellow brick road took us to Atchison, Kansas and Saint Joseph, Missouri. We followed it to Klamath Falls, McNary, and Grants Pass, Oregon, up north to Nampa, Meridian, Boise, and Council, Idaho. It saw the births of two more sons. Our resume expanded to include not only restaurant management but farming, firewood cutting, countertop building, and restaurant ownership. When John tired of a job, or a better offer came along, we relocated.

Accepting a job offer in the Midwest, not long after we reconciled, was doomed from the beginning. Our truck broke down on the way to Kansas, delaying us two days. As we neared our destination, I became concerned when we passed an area devastated by a recent tornado that left trees uprooted and homes destroyed. *Was this decision a mistake?* I wondered. I tried to keep a positive attitude. The home we rented bordered farmland with a field, overgrown with tall grass. When the lights were out and we were cuddled in bed, the house came alive with the sounds of tiny feet scurrying across the linoleum floor. I tried night lights to discourage them, to no avail. I quickly sat up, startled.

"Something just ran across my legs," I told John. I was sure of it. I didn't hear it jump off the bed. I didn't see it. But I was sure I felt it.

"You dreamed it. You're so paranoid," John insisted. I wasn't convinced. *They are harmless mice,* I reminded myself.

Atchison, Kansas was west of the Missouri River. I was hired to manage the Atchison KFC store. Saint Joseph, Missouri sits on the east side of the river, 30 minutes away. John managed that store, and supervised the Atchison store. We were in Atchison for several months when I woke one morning with severe abdominal pains.

"Do you want me to call someone in to work for you?" John offered. I assured him I'd be ok and if I needed to come home, I'd let him know. When I doubled over in pain at work, it frightened my employee.

"Y'all ok?" I could see the panic in her eyes.

"Will you call John and ask him to come over?"

As she called John, I made my way to the restroom. I laid on the floor, pressing my cheek against the coolness on the tile floor, sweat drenching my body. I noticed red spots near the door. I lifted myself to a sitting position, seeing streaks of crimson trickle down my legs. *What is going on?* It scared me. I moved to the toilet. When the door opened, and John walked in, I burst into tears. John helped me to my feet. He flushed the bright red water.

"Let's get you to the doctor."

Concerned about my late cycle when we arrived in Kansas several months earlier, I immediately went to the doctor. The pregnancy exam proved negative. Just a late cycle, that's nothing unusual for me, I felt relieved. In the months I was late, my monthly cramps always seemed more extreme, but nothing as severe as today.

"You've just had a miscarriage, Esther," the doctor informed me after the examination. "It appears you had a tubal pregnancy. That would explain the negative exam when you came in. With tubal pregnancies, the egg has no room to grow and eventually aborts."

John cried at the news. We had just lost a child, one we didn't know we were having. I felt guilty that when I'd received the negative exam early on, I was relieved I wasn't pregnant. With two toddlers, it would be best to wait a little longer to have a third child.

Mice weren't the only things that taunted me in the Midwest. I hated bugs of every kind. Cockroaches multiply in dirty, filthy environments, so I thought. I discovered those disgusting hard-shell creatures, who wiggle their tentacles and move at lightning speed, measuring anywhere from one inch to two inches long, can multiply anywhere. I cringed as I watched them race over the walls of a brand-new home. And though I loved the nightly sounds of crickets when I was growing up, I despised how these little black creatures found their way into the KFC store at night — by the hundreds. I had to tiptoe through the masses, with an occasional crunch under my feet. I swept them out the front door where the live ones could make their escape for another night, leaving the dead ones to be swept into a large black mound and thrown in the trash. The cricket cycle repeated each morning. *It's all a part of living in the Midwest. You'll get used to it.* I assured myself that I'd adjust. It just takes time.

Carrying a 30-pound case of chicken out of the walk-in cooler, I didn't notice the water that dripped from the box. Stepping on the wet slick tile, my feet flew out from under me and my body hurled toward the floor. I dropped the heavy box and, to brace my fall, I threw my arm out. I heard a *CRACK!* A broken wrist, casted from fingertips to mid-forearm, required eight weeks off work.

"Since I'm unable to work for two months, why don't we move

closer to your work?" I hoped John would agree. A move will get us away from the mice infested field. John commuted a half hour to St. Joseph each morning. A move would also save time and expense of travel. He did agree.

I loved the time I spent with the boys while my wrist healed but winter was setting in. Temperatures got colder, and colder, and colder. I'm a sunshine person. *I don't do subzero temperatures well,* I whined to myself... almost daily. The brutal cold kept us mostly inside. The boys begged to play in the snow. Bundled in snow clothes, scarves, stocking hats, and gloves until they could barely move, I'd take them out long enough to make several runs with their sled, down the hill in the backyard. With cherry red noses, we'd go back inside and warm up with hot chocolate, read a book, and find things to play inside for the remainder of the day. Any fantasy of adjusting to the Midwest seemed to bury itself under the snow and ice. I was sick of the cockroaches, the mice, the crickets, and this blasted cold... I wanted to leave it all behind... I wanted to go home! Back to the west coast where a visit with family was only a day's drive away. I spent the better part of one more dreary afternoon crying. My puffy red eyes were tattletales.

"Winter will be over soon." John's attempt to reassure me didn't help, instead it raised my defenses. Afraid he'd say no, I panicked.

"I wanna go home," I sobbed. "I'm going back to the west coast with or without you!"

Blurting an ultimatum wasn't my intention. John didn't argue. He gave notice. The boys and I flew to Oregon. He followed later.

I came, I saw, I made it awkward.

Stephen, John and Larry
Missouri 1975

∞ ∞ ∞

Rabbits, Chickens and Geese, Oh My!

I admired John's audacity to try new things. The type of things I would never try myself. When he posed new ideas, I went along for the ride. Fearfully, but always glad he could take those risks for us. I trusted his judgment. He was the driver. *But farming? – Sure. Why not?* My sister and her family lived in Klamath Falls, Oregon — farming, lumber and rodeo country. For John, finding a farmhouse on five acres was like a little boy getting his first puppy. He sprang into action, researching everything he could about farming. Our chicken coop soon bustled with laying hens and an incubator to keep 100 newborn chicks warm. John answered an ad for a herd of rabbits – delivery and hutches included.

"There's a market for rabbit meat," he assured me. Pulling green chain at the Merrill lumber mill would suffice as the primary income, supplemented by farming – once the farming business took off.

Our farming adventure was a saga worthy of an entire book in itself. John juggled his weekday lumber mill job with farming chores of feeding animals, cleaning cages, butchering rabbit fryers, and tending a garden. I enjoyed the atmosphere of the farm, nature, the sounds of animals, the rooster's crow that woke us each morning, in lieu of an alarm clock. The five acres, one side bordered by an irrigation canal and the other side by a railroad track, became an open range to a pair of ducks, geese, and a mischievous goat. After several days of exploring the home front, both ducks disappeared. Our assumption: the irrigation canal offered a plethora of adventure for them. The geese lasted a little longer. When all three goslings disappeared on the same date, we were convinced the irrigation canal was the culprit, enticing these feathered friends beyond their control. We opted not to replace them, suspecting a repeat performance.

The rabbits were beginning to multiply. The hens were laying, and the chicks were growing. With the incubator turned off, the chicks were free to roam in the large, fenced pen. John was ready to plant a garden. He purchased a rototiller, decided on a location near the barn and began to plow. With one trip around the perimeter of the chosen location, he began working inward as he plowed. I sorted seeds in the covered carport. The dirt and dust clouds hurled around him, collecting on his face and clothes, as the tiller rumbled and vibrated through the soft dry ground. The motor stopped.

"What the #x!#?" I could clearly hear him from where I worked in the carport. His choice words sharply slicing through the air. I saw him lean over and pick something up. He held up the mangled remains of a gosling. Kicking the dirt around, he uncovered the other two. Through inquiries, we discovered a pack of dogs occasionally roam the area. Mysteriously, the predators left no evidence of feathers, blood, or a struggle. We never uncovered the ducks, so we held to our suspicion that the ducks swam the canal.

Billy, our goat, though generally harmless, had a feisty streak. He meandered through the field, keeping the weeds in check. However, he had one major pet peeve: our rambunctious youngsters, ages four and five. When they saw him lying in the grass, they would straddle his back and try to ride him like a horse. Billy would refuse to budge. As I worked in the garden one afternoon, I heard a faint voice calling out.

"Help! Help! Mommy help!" The tone was surprisingly

nonchalant, almost comical. I hurried around the barn to find Larry lying on the ground – Billy lay sprawled across his belly. Larry pushed and prodded, but Billy remained stubborn. I intervened. Grabbing Billy's horns, I tugged. He finally relented, rose to his knees, then hopped to his feet. He lazily sauntered off to the field as if to say, "see how it feels." Larry escaped the ordeal uninjured.

Rabbit litters were born weekly. John was right about the market being good and he butchered rabbit fryers each weekend. We froze some for personal use and sold others. The boys reveled in the freedom to climb fences, trees, and explore the property. When I worried about the little ones taking risks, John would reprimand me.

"Just let them be boys! That's what little boys do." But when Larry took a tumble from the top bunk bed at night and broke his collarbone, John was the one who came unglued.

One of the highlights of the boys' day came from their routine of running out to the yard when they heard the train approaching. As the caboose neared, they'd wave wildly. The conductor, accustomed to their pattern, never failed to be there, standing at the rear and returning the enthusiastic wave.

We welcomed the cackling ruckus of hens which meant we'd have fresh eggs for breakfast. When several days passed with no eggs, we suspected critters were finding their way through the weathered plank siding, stealing the eggs. Repairs were needed and I assisted John with the job. As he steadied a new board against the wall with an outstretched arm, I made a split-second decision to duck under, intending to place myself in a position to better hold the plank. As I did, he raised the hammer, and the claw end caught my upper lip. I felt a stinging pain, my hand grasped my mouth, the blood oozed through my fingers.

John watched from across the room as the doctor sewed the gaping wound. The doctor's demeanor was as cold as the room itself. Trying to break the silence, John joked.

"What would you charge me to stitch the entire mouth shut?" He laughed, trying to lighten the mood. I tried to chuckle, but half of my lip was numbed, and the doctor's pulling and poking with a needle made it near impossible.

"That's not gonna happen." The doctor quietly mumbled, his expression stern in contrast to John's attempt at humor. I sensed the doctor didn't believe our story. I'm sure he'd heard a lot of injury excuses in his line of work. I glanced at John, relieved he didn't hear the doctor's response, nor could he see the doctor's expression that accompanied it. John wouldn't have reacted kindly to any implication of misconduct, a sensitive subject due to an incident several years prior which resulted in an emergency room visit. On that date, during a heated argument, John flung his coffee cup across the room. The ceramic mug shattered as it hit my forehead. I clutched a towel to the pulsating throbs, absorbing the gushing blood flow as we drove 20 miles to the ER to have it stitched shut.

John finished the chicken coop repairs without me and we were once again collecting eggs. It wasn't long, the chicks reached fryer size — time to butcher.

"Let's do 20 at a time," John suggested. He expertly butchered while I tackled the tedious and exhausting job of plucking and preparing the birds for freezing. The summer heat intensified the pungent aroma of raw chicken, making my stomach churn. My fingers ached trying to extricate each little pinfeather. My back screamed in protest of leaning over the sink. I wiped away the trickling sweat from my face, feeling a wave of nausea wash over me. Even with the utility room door open and fans circulating the air, the smell was overpowering. I dragged a chair to the sink, hoping to alleviate my aching back – we were only halfway through the first batch. Leaning over the counter, I rested my head on my arm. Just as I thought I could take a break, John walked in, carrying two more birds, their limp bodies a grim reminder of the many birds yet to come.

"Are you okay, honey?" He put the dead birds in the sink and stood next to my exhausted body. As I looked at him, tears welled in my eyes then slowly rolled down my cheeks.

"I'm sorry. I can't pluck another feather." I cried, feeling as if I were letting him down by not finishing my part of the job. John dismissed that notion and helped me to the living room where I allowed my pregnant body to collapse onto the sofa. John finished the two remaining birds. We kept the already butchered fryers for personal use in our freezer. We sold the remaining fryers as live birds. Our farm stock was reduced to a half dozen layers, lots of rabbits, and a goat… and we had a productive garden.

We made a drive over the mountain pass to spend an evening with my parents for the 4th of July holiday. We arrived home to yet another disaster.

"What the hell?" John exclaimed, leaping out of the car to survey the damage. Rabbit hutches were overturned, doors hung from their hinges. Tufts of fur and mangled rabbits lay scattered across the yard. The pack of dogs had a field day during our absence. Their playful rampage left a trail of destruction. The surviving rabbits cowered in their upright cages, traumatized by the ordeal. The aftermath was just as devastating: litters born in the following weeks were stillborn, or the traumatized mothers devoured their own young after giving birth.

John realized the harsh realities of farming and the emotional toll of chasing that dream. The lumber mill job, mundane and unsatisfying to John, had been continued as a means to support our farming endeavors. Faced with the disillusionment of farming, John talked of leaving the mill and finding a new interest. He sold the remaining rabbits, hutches, and chickens. We gave Billy the Goat away, and harvested the last of the summer garden crop. Then we waited... until that familiar pain poked at my side on September 2, 1976.

"I'm beginning to feel some pain this morning." I told John as he got ready for work. "Do you want to go to work and I'll call if they get stronger?"

"After last time, I'll stay home," he said. Four hours later Christopher was born.

If you never try, you'll never know.

———

Larry, Christopher (11 months),
and Stephen - 1977

∞ ∞ ∞

Chapter Six

The Woodshed

It's hard to pinpoint the exact reason for the euphoria I felt while being in the mountains cutting firewood. Perhaps it's a combination of all that I loved about the woods: the fresh crisp air, filled with the scent of pine needles; the silence, with no traffic, no people; the rustling sound of the breeze as it loosens the colorful array of red, yellow and brown leaves, causing them to gently flutter to the ground; the feeling of being on top of the world as I overlooked the valley below.

I loved the earthy smells after the roar of a chainsaw cracked the silence, whirring its way through the logs. The saw spewed dirt and sawdust, stirring up the pungent smell of oak, the sweet smell of cedar, and the familiar odor of pine. Even a hint of turpentine smell from the pitch that oozed its way out of the wood seemed familiar. Those smells took me back to the woodshed days.

———

"Turn it around. There's pitch on that one." I readjusted the piece of wood, so the pitch faced away from her clothes and skin. I piled firewood on Mary's arms until she exclaimed, "that's enough." She headed for the house as Ronnie returned to the shed, empty handed. He would load my arms, and the chain process continued until the wood box next to the stove overflowed. If we put off our chore until dusk, we would be flailing our arms wildly, desperately trying to shoo away the bats that erratically darted about our heads.

I don't remember Dad bringing home firewood or taking me along to cut it. I do recall our woodshed was always full — and filled with the earthy aromas I grew to love — the aromas that sparked the memories during my firewood-cutting days with John. For several months, our income came from cutting, selling and stacking firewood for a mere $55 per cord, until the harsh winter weather made the roads impassable. It was hard work, yet something I loved doing.

Those memories drew me back to the woods years later when I found myself volunteering with the firewood cutting ministry at River Valley Community Church.

The best memories in life can never be captured by
pictures, they are only captured by the heart.

∞∞∞

A Wish Come True

I remember watching 11 month-old, Christopher, play in the front yard while listening to music on the radio. The announcer stopped the song. I couldn't believe what I heard next. "The King is Dead." I was devastated. It was August 16, 1977, when I heard the breaking news. I had been a huge fan of Elvis Presley since junior high school, mesmerized by his music and charisma. His hit song, "Heartbreak Hotel" topped the charts in 1956, when I was just six years old. After serving in the army, Elvis continued to defy the controversy of his wild, sensual stage presence and became known as the King of Rock and Roll. Now the iconic figure was gone.

We were living in McNary, Oregon at that time — an unincorporated community along the Columbia River on the outskirts of Umatilla. John often took the two older boys fishing at the base of McNary dam, where six-foot sturgeon could be spotted, though illegal to catch.

John and I worked for Tom Peters, building countertops. I also assisted Tom with installations in the homes. One morning I leaned over the front office counter, feeling a little faint. I continued to review the paperwork for our next order. In an instant, the room went dark. I could hear a faint voice.

"Are you ok? Esther, are you ok?" It was John's voice.

When I opened my eyes, I saw a blurry Tom standing over me. John was kneeling beside me, asking again if I was ok. My head throbbed but, other than the egg I felt when I rubbed my hand across the back of my head, I seemed to be ok.

Eight months later, I found myself lying in a hospital bed surrounded by nurses in those familiar starched, blue scrubs. I followed the nurse's instructions to the letter. I sat up, swung my legs over the side of the gurney, and leaned forward, trying to relax.

"Whatever you do, don't sit up straight," she cautioned. My body betrayed me as it involuntarily shot straight up, into a sitting position, and I let out an ear-piercing scream as the needle entered my low back. Fortunately for me, the needle didn't snap. Within minutes, the epidural took effect, numbing my pelvic area, and I was wheeled into a bright, sterile room. Though their faces were masked, I recognized the kind eyes of Dr. Johnson, my family doctor. His presence was a reassuring constant during a time of chaos. After examining me that afternoon, he informed me that surgery was necessary and, though he was not a surgeon, he would certainly be there to assist.

"Would you like to stay awake during the procedure?" the doctor asked me.

"Yes, if that's possible."

I liked Dr. Johnson from the date of my first appointment, months ago. It was extremely awkward having my feet propped in stirrups when this young doctor entered the room. He smiled, introduced himself, and made friendly conversation as he settled himself on a chair at my feet. I tried to make light of the situation in spite of my embarrassment.

"I hate these pelvic exams," I told him. "The metal on the clamp is always so cold." He peered at me over the sheet that covered my knees, giving a little modesty barrier between us. He chuckled. Then the next thing he said made me laugh out loud.

"Oh, it won't be cold," he said, "Since you can't see me, I'll tuck it under my armpit to warm it up for you." His bedside manner showed professionalism yet gave the feeling that we'd been friends for years.

I watched the busy movements of the masked surgeons above the shield that restricted vision of the surgery itself. Dr. Johnson made eye contact on occasion, asking if I was ok. It seemed the procedure was over in minutes when he asked me,

"Should I throw in the towel? It's a boy!"

"I'll keep him!" The anesthetist placed a mask over my mouth and nose. The room plunged into darkness.

Dr. Johnson and I had a running joke that he would be certain to deliver a girl. At this point in his young career, he had only delivered girls. I later suggested that maybe this delivery wouldn't count in those calculations since it was not a normal birth, but cesarean. After labor started that morning, I went to the hospital. During the examination, the doctor determined the baby changed positions and was now breech, requiring emergency surgery.

When I awoke from the anesthesia, my body trembled violently. My clenched fists grasped the bedrails causing them to rattle as I struggled to curb the shaking. After what seemed an eternity, a nurse poked her head into the doorway.

"You're awake," she said.

"Yes... can you please give me something to stop the shaking?" I managed to whisper. My strength seemed to be zapped from the uncontrollable trembling. I felt embarrassed to be asking but my entire body ached as it shook. I was desperate for relief.

"Oh, don't be such a baby." The nurse's response was curt. I turned my face away. Ashamed for asking, I didn't want to make eye contact. I continued to grip the rails – they continued to rattle as she briefly checked my incision, then left the room, not another word. She didn't bring anything for relief. I rode the storm without it.

Dr. Johnson sat near my bed early the next morning while making his rounds. He lowered his voice to a near whisper to keep our conversation private,

"John came to see you last night while you were still in recovery. The staff turned him away." He went on to say John got belligerent when told he couldn't see me until I came out of recovery. They could smell alcohol on his breath and asked him to leave. John refused and security was called to assist.

John panicked when he found out the baby was breech and that surgery was necessary.

"What if something happens to you or the baby during surgery?" He mentioned the miscarriage in Kansas. I tried to convince him that I would be in good hands, and he had nothing to worry about. Though the surgery went well, they placed Duane in an incubator to correct signs of yellow jaundice, a common symptom of cesarean births.

After being turned away at the hospital, John went home and demolished several pieces of living room furniture when he threw them through the apartment window. Five days later, Duane and I were released from the hospital. The window and broken furniture had been replaced. Other than John briefly saying "I took my stress out on the window," further discussion was avoided. I never told him I was aware he was removed from the hospital by security.

Since birth control pills were not free in my childbearing days, and I worked long hours, it was difficult to get an appointment to get the prescription renewed. I tended to run out. If I missed a pill, I seemed to get pregnant.

"Call me Miss Fertile Myrtle," I'd joke with people. After Duane's birth I opted for an intrauterine device for future prevention.

"Don't you want to try once more for a girl?" John asked. I knew John would be happy with ten children.

"You have a son from your first marriage. We have four sons. What makes you think we'd have a girl next time?" I laughed and dismissed his suggestion of "one more try."

Once during my fourth pregnancy, as I walked through the store with three little boys in tow, someone approached me and made a comment:

"You must be a good Catholic or Mormon."

"Nope – I just want four kids," I responded flatly.

As a teenager, I always said my wish was to someday have three little boys. That wish came true, plus one. In my mind, I suspect my miscarriage may have been my girl. I won't know that answer until I reach Heaven's gates.

God's ways are indeed mysterious. While working for Tom, we lacked health insurance, but our move to Grants Pass, Oregon during my pregnancy, brought new opportunities. John quickly found work with the forest service and later at Diamond Industries, a large cabinet manufacturer. Fortunately, Diamond Industries offered health insurance, effective from day one of employment. However, since my pregnancy pre-existed John's employment start date, the birth would not qualify for coverage. When Dr. Johnson recommended a cesarean section, I worried about the hospital and surgery bills. Once I was home from the hospital and recuperated, I received a call from him.

"The surgeon submitted his bills to the insurance company and they paid the entire bill," he told me. When I inquired of the insurance company, I discovered that emergency surgery was indeed covered, therefore, the insurer paid the entire hospital and surgery bills, leaving us with only the initial in-office doctor visits. We were truly grateful for this unexpected blessing.

Sometimes I look up, smile, and say,
"I know that was You, God.
Thank you.

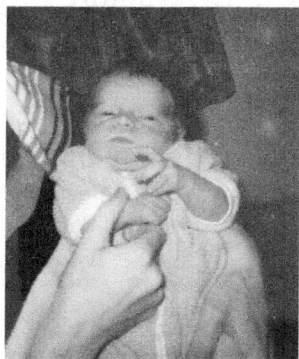
Duane - 11 days old

∞ ∞ ∞

The Grubstake
a Family Affair

"**A**nnette, would you like to see how my boots hurt when I kick?" With the questioning grin of a four-year-old, Duane's head tilted up to see the face of this towering, large framed woman. Annette, our breakfast cook, showed up to work each morning dressed in boots and blue jeans. I stood by, wide eyed at his request, waiting with anticipation to see how this would play out.

Too young for school, Duane, the youngest of our four sons, spent his days at the restaurant with us. When Duane pulled on his brown, pointed toe cowboy boots, he was like a superhero changing into uniform. His personality transformed. He no longer walked; he strutted across the room. He stood straight, his chin lifted high. He kicked everything he walked past, testing the strength of his first pair of boots.

Annette turned and looked down at this little guy, not even waist high to her. She glanced in my direction then back at him. *I'm glad he at least asked before he acted,* I thought. Annette's face went serious as she firmly planted her hands on her hips. She leaned over, face inches from Duane's, her squinted eyes gave an are-you-daring-me look.

"Do you... young man... want to see how *my* boots hurt... when *I* kick?" Her words were slow and assertive.

"No." A pouty lip went out and his smile disappeared.

"Then run along and play," her voice was light and playful this time. Her hand gave a get-along little cowboy type of wave as she motioned him out of the kitchen. Once out of our sight, our laughter erupted.

Council was a tiny town in the mountains, two hours northwest of Boise, Idaho, not far from the popular ski resort area of McCall. Population 1,000. John and I signed a one-year lease on the full-service restaurant located inside a huge, historic, brick hotel. The hotel itself had been vacant for many years.

The offer of the lease came to us unexpectedly. We had finally settled down. With the boys in school, it wasn't feasible to be on the move continuously. Nearly four years had passed since John accepted the job as District Manager for the Red Steer Corporation, owned by the Hawkins brothers. The longest tenure in one place since we'd married. As District Manager, he supervised the corporation's chain of KFC and Red Steer (hamburger) units. I managed one of the KFC Stores.

We purchased a three-bedroom, one-bath rambler house on an extra-large lot in the suburbs of Boise. With no fence, our spacious yard became the neighborhood playground. I became a member of the Nazarene Church in Meridian. One evening John came home with a cat caught the mouse grin.

"I got a call about a restaurant for lease in Council. We need to check it out!" John spoke fast, his voice filled with excitement. His hazel eyes sparkled. I recognized that look.

"Is the corporation thinking about buying it?" I quizzed, hopeful that's where he was going with this. They, at one time in the past, bought a steakhouse and had John open it.

"No. I think it would be the perfect business for us. It's a small community. The restaurant serves breakfast, lunch and dinner... full service, not fast food." John continued to talk rapidly. That was usually an indication he'd made up his mind.

I knew John's dream was to have a successful business, any kind of business, of his own. Regardless, the idea caught me off guard. We were finally settled. There had been some major changes in the company that concerned him. Hearing this idea, I suspected he had been watching for opportunities. His expertise was food service, so the restaurant idea made sense.

John's tall, slender frame and thick dark hair, complete with stylish '80s sideburns, made him a handsome figure. The scar across his cheek added a hint of ruggedness to his appearance. As he worked with teenage girls and female managers, it was no secret that they found him charming. Their flirtatious behavior was often met with playful responses from John, which occasionally sparked my jealousy. However, I recognized that his charm was an inherent part of his personality, and I learned to navigate those feelings. When he got enthusiastic about something, like this restaurant idea, his boyish excitement was infectious and irresistible even to me.

"It's a small town. You'll get to know everyone."

John was kind, courteous and professional when he interacted with customers and, though his customers loved him, he had no interest in socializing outside of work. Seeing my desire for interaction with ladies at my church, he recognized my need. His high energy enthusiasm spilled over to me. It always did eventually. We drove the two hours to Council to check it out. We fell in love with the quaint town, and the old brick historic hotel building. The Grubstake restaurant and the Ace Saloon shared the building.

One main street with most of the buildings connecting side by side, gave the appearance of a small town in a western movie. Businesses included a hardware store, general store, and a gift shop, a few small businesses, a schoolhouse, and a county courthouse. And, on the outskirts of town, a small Nazarene church. We signed a one-year lease with an option to renew.

"We can move the mobile home up there," John told me when I questioned about housing. Prior to buying our Boise home, we purchased a 14'x70' mobile home, with an 8'x13' expanded living room. We lived in it a short while on a parcel of land in Eagle, a community outside Boise. When we bought the house, we rented out the mobile. We placed the mobile on a lot only three blocks from the restaurant in Council. We leased the Boise house to a young couple for one year.

June 1981 marked the grand opening of the Grubstake, our dream restaurant. With two cooks and two waitresses on board, we were ready to tackle the busy times of day. John and I worked full-time, leaving little time for socializing outside of work. I did get to know the locals well, as they became our loyal customers. A few months after opening, the local economy took a downturn. The Boise Cascade mill and local silver mine closed, a first in history, we were told. Business slowed and we cut back to one waitress to help me and kept the two cooks on board. Some customers ordered breakfast, but others spent a quarter on a cup of coffee and drank a full pot while they chatted for hours with other customers. It was a challenging time.

The usual group of guys gathered around their table one morning,

"I'll have my regular," one customer said.

"And that is…." my eyebrow raised as I questioned.

"My Leo cakes!" a surprised, slightly indignant, answer came back to me. Leo didn't like the larger sized pancakes we served. He liked small silver dollar sized cakes. We began calling them Leo Cakes and other customers began ordering Leo Cakes. I leaned in closer, studying his face.

"Leo! I didn't recognize you without your hat!" An almost rhythmic howl came from the group of men sitting at the table as I tasseled the few hairs on Leo's bare head. Leo was noted for the yellow fishing style bucket hat he wore.

The boys became instant hits with customers. They mingled amongst the tables, visiting with the regulars. During the slower hours when only John and I worked, the boys would bus tables, help run the dishwasher, and tackle small jobs such as peeling potatoes and grating cheese. This close-knit cowboy town had an air of safety and comfort. We allowed the boys to play in the tiny park, adjacent to the Grubstake... without supervision. They did their homework and played games in the huge storage room. They had the run of the vacant upstairs hotel rooms. There was no lack of entertainment for them.

Cutting back on a waitress meant I worked until ten o'clock when we closed at night. For that reason we started closing at eight o'clock. There wasn't a lot of business after that time. We had a few disgruntled customers when we also decided to close our doors on Sundays, but it gave us one day for family.

Whether we were blessed, or John's reputation preceded him, another offer came at an appropriate time... not long before our lease was to expire.

"Would you be interested in a breakfast and lunch house or are you pretty well settled in Council?" Claire Hawkins, one of the Hawkins Brothers who owned the Red Steer Corporation, called John.

"What do you have in mind?" John questioned.

"The Trolley House is available for lease. It's a small but booming breakfast and lunch cafe in downtown Boise. We'd love to have you in there."

We finished out our lease with the Grubstake and moved back to our home in Boise, June 1982. The Trolley House posed the perfect schedule for me and John. Breakfast and lunch would be served in this quaint building, fashioned to look like a trolley station, with summer hours 6 a.m. to 4 p.m. Clientele consisted of early morning golfers on their way to the nearby course. Families came in for lunch when they spent the day cooling off in the water at the hydrotube water slide next door. Other customers were employees of the government offices close by who came in during their lunch hour. Winter hours, when the hydrotube closed, would be 6 a.m. - 2 p.m. Since the cafe was located in the government district of downtown Boise, there was no market for a dinner hour. Our evenings would be free for family time. With seating capacity less than 100 and open only daytime hours, John and I could operate this cafe with minimal staff. Golfers stood outside the door each morning waiting for me to unlock at 6 a.m. The 99-cent breakfast — two eggs, hashbrowns and toast — was a hot seller. At the end of our first week, we knew this would be the ideal restaurant for us...

...until the phone rang.

———

"You are never too old to set another goal
or to dream a new dream."
C.S. Lewis

∞ ∞ ∞

The Grubstake - Council, Idaho - 1981-1982

Chapter Seven

The Phone Call

"I'm going to keep the boys home today," I told John. I gave no explanation. He shrugged, picked up his coffee, and went out the door. It was July 8, 1982. John and I were up early. I would go to the Trolley House while John made a trip to Council to pick up the last of our personal items. He planned to take the two older boys with him.

John liked to read in the evening. It helped him unwind after a busy day. When he got particularly interested in a book, he'd stay up late until he finished it. It wasn't unusual for him to get by on little sleep. He came to bed at 3 a.m. When I walked into the living room at 5 a.m. I picked up several beer cans, wrinkling my nose at their stale pungent odor. I emptied the ashtray, full of nicotine butts. When John went to wake the boys, I followed my gut feeling, *He hasn't had much sleep. Don't let the boys ride with him.* I kept them home and John drove to Council alone.

That evening, as the boys ran off their energy outside, I prepared dinner. The phone made several shrill rings before I picked up the receiver.

"I'm calling from Saint Alphonsus hospital. Is this Esther?" My chest grew heavy with dread, a deja vu moment, remembering the last time I got a call from the hospital. "Your husband was in an auto accident. He is being transported here by ambulance and should be here within the hour." That's all she could, or was willing, to tell me. My neighbor agreed to keep watch on the boys. I arrived at the hospital, not knowing what was in store.

"The ambulance will be here soon," the desk clerk informed me. Then she pointed toward the waiting room.

"Someone is waiting for you."

We'd been back in Boise for only a month. That time had been consumed with getting the Trolley House ready to open. *Who would know we are back? How would they know about the accident?* Alberta Rhodes stood up, arms open wide to embrace me, as I walked into the waiting room. Before I could speak, she explained.

"Ron got a call. They said John was in an accident and they didn't know how to locate you. They told us he was being transported here. I didn't know how to reach you so I just came."

Ron Rhodes was the pastor of the Nazarene Church I attended before moving to Council. Alberta is his wife.

"The ambulance is just pulling in," a nurse said, poking her head in the waiting room. I was allowed to follow alongside John as they rushed him to emergency. A weak smile crossed his face before he closed his eyes again. Alberta stayed with me, praying for a positive outcome. In the meantime, a Sheriff's deputy arrived.

"I have a few questions so I can complete my report." I gave him our updated contact information and answered other questions; where he was headed, the reason for the trip. With his report complete, he relayed the miraculous unfolding of details, per witness accounts. The accident report confirmed the story I hazily recalled him telling me:

The two-lane road between Boise and Council wound through farmland and hills, passing the little towns of Fruitvale and Weiser. Driving southbound from Council, a witness, following behind John, noticed John's truck weaving, then veering off the pavement onto the right shoulder. Hitting the gravel, the truck bolted back to the left, shot across both lanes, and hit the embankment on the other side.

"We suspect he fell asleep at the wheel," the officer said. The impact with the embankment flipped John's truck, causing it to roll back across both lanes. It rolled over the front of an oncoming vehicle, and into a ravine before it came to an abrupt stop. The driver of the other vehicle was a young sailor, home on leave. He reported that he rounded the corner and saw the truck coming toward him. In an instant, he threw himself across the front seat of his vehicle. He survived with a few scrapes and bruises. As John's truck hit the ravine, he was thrown head first through the windshield.

The driver who had been following John provided a crucial eyewitness account. She stated that John stood up, walked to the edge of the road, then suddenly collapsed. The witness was a registered nurse, and she immediately provided medical attention. When another vehicle approached, she quickly instructed the driver to go call for help. In a stroke of luck, within a short distance, the driver came across a police officer who had pulled over a speeding car. The officer radioed for emergency assistance, and help was soon on the way.

But who called the church? I wondered. The miracle — or coincidence for those who don't believe in miracles —

continues:

Council is a small town where everyone knows everyone. I attended church with the local game warden. He and his family were customers of ours at the Grubstake. John was unconscious by the time paramedics reached him. There was no contact information in his wallet. His driver's license still possessed the Council address. The sheriff's department, out of Weiser, was unaware of how to reach me. Being tuned in on the scanner, my game warden friend heard the conversation, and the name John Stark. He sprang into action.

"They recently moved back to Boise. Contact the Meridian Nazarene Church. I know Esther used to attend there. They might know how to reach her."

I had not been to the church yet as we'd been tied up with getting the Trolley house open. Receiving the call, Alberta immediately drove to the hospital to be there when I arrived. While Alberta and I waited, another source of information arrived. The paramedic stopped by the waiting room to see how I was doing.

"He's one lucky guy," the paramedic said, "he flatlined three times on the way here, but his vitals were strong by the time we arrived."

Call it lucky, or call the entire sequence a miracle, I thought to myself. It was several hours before the doctor came in. He spoke bluntly and to the point. John was conscious when he came in; is now heavily sedated, and…

"Your husband has a broken neck. He will never walk again." I sat in shock… and denial.

"Of course he will. John can do anything he sets his mind to," I objected.

"He'll never walk again," the doctor repeated coldly as he went out the door.

Everything happens for a reason. Sometimes
it hurts, sometimes it's hard.

Lending a Helping Hand

"If you need anything at all, please call me." I received numerous offers, but I felt uncomfortable saying I needed help. Instead, I lied.

"I'm doing ok." The truth was far from it. My workday started at 5 a.m., opening the cafe at 6 a.m. I'd lock up at 4 p.m. leaving an employee to finish the closing chores. I picked up the boys and drove to the hospital for an hour or more. I'd return home, feed the boys, go to bed and start all over again. Chores at home began to pile up.

John lay strapped to a Stryker board, with a vice grip contraption holding a weight that hung from his skull. It prevented him from turning his neck. For three long weeks, he was trapped in this position. After several hours they'd place another board over him — this one with a cutout for his face. They would unhook the vice grip from his head and, like a Belgian waffle maker, they flipped him over. This process relieved the pressure from his backside. Each evening I'd visit and find him face down, staring at the floor through the hole in the board. I'd sit on the floor to see his face, but making eye contact was hopeless. One nurse, seeing me lying on the floor, propped on my elbow, commented,

"Well, that's a little awkward. Let's see what we can do about that." I told her my typical visiting schedule and she arranged his rotation to match my schedule. The boys would greet their dad, then head to the waiting room, where books, toys, and puzzles made their time pass enjoyably. The neighbor offered to keep them during my hospital visit but I wanted their dad to see them.

I didn't know how to accept an offer of help, much less ask for help. After closing the Trolley House one afternoon I drove home to get the boys. I saw several cars parked in front of our rambler style house. Three men were in the yard when I pulled into the driveway, and I saw a woman standing inside through the living room window. Tears burst to the surface as I sat in the car, unable to move. One man walked to the car and opened my door.

"We called and your son said it was ok to come over."

"It is. Of course it is!" I could barely manage the words.

Another man grinned broadly and waved as he drove our old lawn mower across the lawn. He seemed to enjoy himself on that old dilapidated thing. Another knelt by the overgrown rose bushes, clippers in hand, a pile of cuttings beside him. He gave a nod hello as I looked in his direction.

The woman held a spray bottle and paper towels in her hands. The windows were squeaky clean. The house was vacuumed and dusted. A large stack of laundry, neatly folded, covered one end of the sectional. I recognized one lady from church. She embraced me with a firm, silent hug. When I regained my composure, she looked me in the eyes.

"I'm going to be stopping by on Saturday mornings for the next few weeks to pick up the laundry. Okay?" Her question was more of a statement. "So don't worry about doing it during the week." She not only laundered them, but I also noted some items were returned mended.

When I told John about it, he said several guys had stopped in at the hospital to "see how you're doing," talked a few minutes and left. He didn't know them.

"Kurt and Sandy came by today," he told me one evening. "I'm surprised you didn't tell them I accepted the Lord." Sandy ran a daycare in Meridian and watched our boys prior to our buying the house in Boise. We became friends, and she introduced me to the Meridian Nazarene Church. Once we'd moved into Boise the distance made it difficult to take them to her. We remained friends. John came home later than usual one evening. I could smell beer on him, but he'd walked in the house with a smile on his face.

"I just accepted the Lord," he told me. I don't recall my words of response. It took me by surprise, and I suspected it might be beer talk. He never wanted to attend church with "so many hypocrites," he'd say. Though he didn't attend, when the boys balked at going, he'd say, "You know that on Sunday mornings when you get up, you're going to church with your mom. I don't want to hear any complaints." Another time he'd told me, "I like Sundays because you always come home from church happy." Two weeks after he'd said he accepted the Lord, he had his accident. The accident that changed his life forever.

After a month on the Stryker bed, the doctor performed surgery to relieve pressure of a vertebrae pressing on the spinal cord, then moved him to a rehabilitation hospital.

"He's a classic case," rehab doctors told me. "With his injury level, he should be a quadriplegic. He's not. His body functions like that of a paraplegic." With another month of summer before school started, my younger sister, Julie, called,

"We're coming to get the boys and bring them home with us. We'll bring them back before school starts." Julie lived in Klamath Falls, Oregon with her husband and three children. They had acreage with a few farm animals. The boys would enjoy being there, I knew that, but it was hard to let them go. I did, at her insistence.

I realized when people offer to help in a time of need, their intentions are genuine. Seldom are they just being nice, which is what I feared. I've since learned to accept offers of help when it makes my life easier. It also taught me to keep my eyes open. When I see a need, I remind myself not everyone knows how to accept an offer of help… if it seems appropriate, take action, pay it forward. The giver is equally blessed as the receiver.

Somewhere along the way
we must learn that there is nothing greater
than to do something for others.
Martin Luther King, Jr.

———

∞ ∞ ∞

Transforming Tragedy

In my opinion, too often John let his pride cloud his better judgment. Prior to his accident — and again after he regained self-sufficiency — if he struggled with something, he'd refuse to seek help. If I suggested such an idea, he'd snap at me.

"I don't need help from anyone." The bristle of his body always reminded me it was not something I should have suggested. He never liked asking anyone for anything. He was too full of pride for that. He had a fiery temper that seethed just below the surface. A stranger bumping into him in a crowded room could cause his temper to erupt, ready for an instant fight. Turn the coin over and he'd be the first to help someone in need. One afternoon we were running late to reach our destination when John flipped his signal on and pulled to the side of the road. Annoyed and impatient, I protested,

"We have to be there in half an hour!"

"We'd want someone to help if it were us." His voice had no hint of negotiation. We saw a car parked along the road a mile back. Now we came upon a man carrying a gas can.

"Hop in," John said, "we'll get you to a station." Not only did we get him to a station several miles down the road, John also drove him back to his car. Helping someone in need became his priority. My frustration turned into quiet shame — at my initial reaction — as I watched the appreciation on the man's face.

John, a man hell bent to do things on his own, who once taught his sons to tie their shoes, who pushed the bicycle as his sons learned to ride, now relied on them to push his wheelchair, to tie his laces. He had to learn patience and adjust to the life restrictions posed by paraplegia. He could no longer refuse help from another, in fact for the first six months at home, he required the assistance of me and the boys to dress, bathe, get in and out of his wheelchair, and drive him to appointments. Reaching items on shelves, retrieving something he dropped, were major challenges. I'm convinced the humility of it all gave John the strength and determination to recover as quickly as he did.

"Esther, come here, hurry!" I dropped what I was doing and responded to the urgency in John's voice. I ran to the living room. John sat in his recliner, feet propped up, a huge grin on his face.

"Watch!" I watched, and waited, not sure what he wanted me to see but sighing a relief that he seemed to be ok.

"Just wait." If one can grimace and grin at the same time, John did. After what seemed like a very long time, he exclaimed, "See it?" the toes on his left foot moved ever so slightly. John persevered, taking back the duties of his personal care one by one. Control of movement in his lower extremities increased somewhat. He regained the sensation of touch to his legs, but was unable to detect the sharpness of a pin prick or the temperature of bath water.

"It's much like the feeling of Novocaine after a dentist visit," he described it to me.

The sensitivity of the scar that stretched from his right shoulder blade, crossing his back and ending just above the left hip bone ended our typical spoon sleeping position. Any touch or bump to that area created muscle spasms throughout his body. Tiny pieces of windshield glass sometimes festered and worked its way out of his back and his scalp.

A monumental day came when his Pontiac Grand Am was parked in the driveway, equipped with adaptive hand controls, empowering him with the freedom of driving.

The Trolley House was our dream restaurant. But, it quickly became clear that John would never be able to operate the business hands-on due to the kitchen's inaccessibility for his wheelchair. We had envisioned it as being the perfect venture for us, with maybe one or two additional employees to help us run it full-time. However, John's expertise far surpassed mine, and in his absence, I discovered I needed more employees than we initially anticipated. He tried to supervise remotely from home, but that didn't sit well with me. I'd already been running the business without his help for several months, while he was in the hospital. My defense antennas were much too sensitive, and suggestions were often taken as personal criticism, causing friction between us. We decided it would be best for him to step back and let me operate at my own discretion. Though I struggled with some of the one-on-one, manager-to-employee skills, I was pleased with the booming business.

———

"If I can't work in food service any more, I might as well get a degree," John told me when I arrived home from work, "as soon as I'm strong enough." That familiar gleam was in his eyes. I was glad he had a plan, something to look forward to. He began researching possibilities, his motivation to overcome his adversities even stronger than before.

John had always been a workaholic, with little time for hobbies. He enjoyed fishing and hunting. One of our favorite things to do on weekends was take the boys to Sage Hen Reservoir to fish. The path from the parking lot to his favorite fishing spot was hard, packed dirt. It meandered through the woods, along the lake's shoreline. Much of the path was sloped. I'd be loaded down with folding chairs, the younger boys with tackle boxes, and we all carried fishing poles. As the path sloped more, Larry and Stephen would have to hold onto John's chair, one pushing over the rocks and bumps, one walking alongside to keep his wheelchair from tipping over with the slope. There was one ravine that required the boys to get John across, having to use all their 12 and 13 year-old strength to keep him upright.

John used a Roho cushion in his wheelchair. It's a rubberized cushion made of bubbles, like individual balloons, each inflated with air. They are designed to prevent pressure sores, since wheelchair users often have poor blood circulation — and they are expensive. As we crossed the ravine, the chair shifted and the boys lost their grip. John tumbled from his chair, and the wheelchair slid toward the lake, stopping at the bank. The pillow, however, flew into the water and began to float away. The boys were concerned about John, trying to upright him. John was concerned more about the expensive pillow, yelling, "Get my pillow, get my pillow." The pillow and chair were recovered, set on level ground and the boys lifted their father into the chair. It was a chaotic beginning to the day but we continued on to the fishing hole, set up our chairs, and fished. I typically watched. I didn't have as much patience for lake fishing. John and the boys had a stringer of fish staked in the water near the bank. Several fishermen passed by, always asking "catch anything?" to which John always answered, "not a bite!" They'd travel down the path to find a good fishing hole. I was troubled by his response. *Usually fishermen brag about their catch!* I thought.

"Why didn't you want to show him your fish?" I asked.

"If they know we're catching fish, they'll crowd right in here next to us."

———

When you work in food service, there are certain customers who are specifically your customers. I'm sure that's probably true with most service-oriented businesses. They want you to wait on them. Much like the group of breakfast and coffee drinkers at the Grubstake, the Trolley House presented the same. I had a number of customers who came in and sat at specific tables, so I would wait on them.

Stan and Dick were two of those customers who came to the Trolley House. They worked at a nearby national grocery warehouse and they held their morning meeting over breakfast.

"If you ever want to leave all this behind, Esther," Stan motioned around the room, "call me. I'll have a job for you." My exhaustion must have been visible one morning because he repeated his offer.

"Are you actually serious?" I sighed. "Because one of these days I just might take you up on the offer."

"Yes, I'm serious!" his voice filled with surprise and he looked at me questioningly, waiting.

"I'll definitely give it some thought." I smiled and gave a thank you wink. I was pleased that someone would offer me a job, without me having to apply.

The Trolley House was a little gold mine for us. It paid off all the debt's accumulated while trying to keep the Grubstake alive. But, I wasn't sure I wanted to renew the lease for another year. I talked with John about terminating the lease at the conclusion, in light of the job offer. We would have health insurance if I worked elsewhere. When our lease ended, I went to work for Stan as a receptionist and was soon promoted to accounts receivables. John's physical condition improved, and he enrolled at the ITT Technical Institute, for a two-year electronic engineering degree.

Idaho's winters were notorious for dumping inches, if not feet, of snow on the ground. The winters didn't change over the years, each being as cold and icy as the previous year. Winter conditions are not the best for maneuvering in a wheelchair. One bone chilling afternoon John seemed agitated when he came home from school.

"Is everything ok?" I asked. I knew four hours of classes were exhausting for him.

"It was a shitty day!"

"What happened?"

"I missed my first class. I had trouble getting out of the car in the snow, then I got stuck in the snow and ice on the sidewalk. Everyone was already in class by then so I sat there for an hour. When the class was dismissed, someone saw me and helped." We discussed our options that night. After nearly eight years in Idaho, we would make a change. Once he graduated, we would move to a warmer location, one more conducive to a wheelchair user. Spring of 1986 John received his degree with a 4.0 gpa. We relocated to Simi Valley, California.

Humility is the ability to give up your pride and still retain your dignity.

————

∞ ∞ ∞

Larry, John, Stephen, Duane, Chris - 1983

∞ ∞ ∞

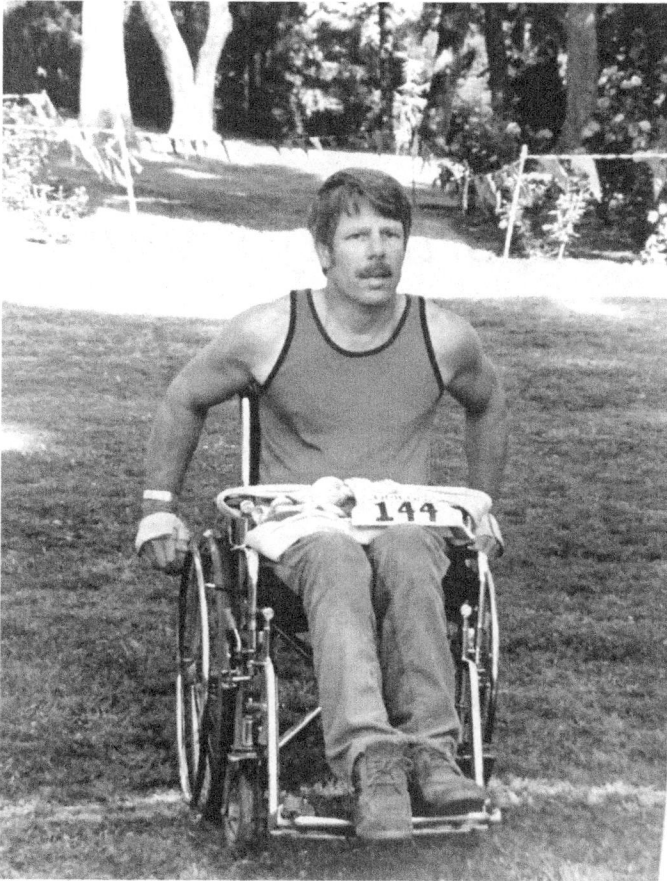

John competed in a 5k fun race - 1988

Chapter Eight

Opportunity Knocks

"I'm their token handicapped person." John said. If it bothered him, he hid it well. He worked the swing shift at an electronics firm. Employees consisted of many Asians, a handful of whites, and one disabled person, being John. His body bore the brunt of the eight-hour shifts. John tried to ignore the signs, excited to be working again.

I immediately went to work through a temporary agency but I continued to search the classifieds for a permanent job.

"This ad sounds interesting." I read it to John. *Executive Secretary for an Engineering Firm. Apply to L. Liston & Associates in Westlake Village.*

"You should apply!"

"I wouldn't qualify." Oh how I wished I did. After three years with the ten-key calculator in accounts receivable, those skills were well advanced but my typing, though quite good in high school, had been sparsely used in recent years.

"You won't know unless you try." The edginess in John's voice relayed his annoyance at my defeated attitude. At his coaxing, I mailed my resume. *I'll probably never hear from them so why not?* Several days later, I sat up waiting for John to get home from work.

"Guess, what. I have an interview tomorrow with that engineering firm." I was excited, and nervous at the same time, about the prospect of this job. I went to the interview with guarded expectations. She hired me on the spot.

I started the job immediately as the secretary to 13 male engineers. I answered phone calls, scheduled appointments, copied blueprints, and typed up civil, architectural, and soil engineer reports. I loved the job. And, because of my history with guy friends, I felt comfortable in this all-male office. Leonard, the owner, preferred working in the field. His procrastination of returning to the office before five o'clock made it difficult to get reports done.

"Mr. Collier called today wanting to know when he'll get his report. I told him you've been out in the field this week but we'd get it done soon."

"Can you stay late tonight?" He'd ask apologetically. Working late three or four times a week became the norm. I didn't mind. The overtime pay was good.

"What was the last thing I said?" Leonard would ask as he paced back and forth behind me. Then he would lean over my shoulder and check the computer screen, confirming what I had read back to him. We didn't use a Dictaphone. Instead, he dictated the report from handwritten notes he had jotted down while in the field. We'd work until he was satisfied. The next morning I'd print out the report, bind it, and call the client for pick up.

Leonard had been putting off, and I had been stalling the client, on one particular report due to its complexity. Another day, another call, another stall. I could sense the client's growing frustration. He was anxious to get the report so he could move forward with his project, but he never spoke a harsh word; he remained calm and understanding. When Leonard came in at five o'clock, he saw the gigantic bouquet of 20 red roses. I placed the bouquet on the file cabinet when it arrived that day.

"Wow! What's the occasion?" He glanced at me, smiling.

"Read the card." I grinned, pointing to the tiny greeting card attached to the bouquet. It read:

"Leonard, Roses are red, violets are blue. I sure would like my report from you." It was signed by the understanding client. Leonard and I stayed late that night, completed the report and had it delivered to the client the next morning.

Shelley, Leonard's wife, did the bookkeeping from home. She popped in and out of the office sporadically. I was surprised at her comment one day as we visited.

"There were two things that jumped out at me on your resume and letter," she said. "The first was that you had your own small business. That meant you knew how small businesses run. The second thing, you have four sons. I knew right then you'd be able to work in an office full of guys! I was sure I would hire you when you came in."

Being the oldest person in the office, at age 36, I quickly acquired the nickname of Mom from the guys. I fit in; I felt accepted; I was good at my job — and, for once, I knew it! If John had not urged me to apply for the job, I would have listened to the negative voice that told me "You don't qualify, Esther" — translated in my mind as *You're not good enough.* I would have missed out on that ideal job. I was surprised to see how personal characteristics play into job qualifications.

The engineering work fascinated me. Amongst our many jobs,

we engineered projects for a lot of well known names – actors, actresses, and singers. Their contractors dealt with our office. Singer Bobby Vinton was an exception. He liked being involved in every aspect of his project and called regularly. I never commented, or asked him, about his career since that wasn't the subject of his calls.

Jingle, Jingle. The bell notified me as the front door *o*pened. A sophisticated, well-dressed man entered. His fair skin, dishwater blonde hair, and pleasant smile rendered him quite handsome. I stood and shook his outreached hand as he introduced himself. Standing in excess of six feet, he towered over my desk.

"I have a project that needs some engineering," he said. I told him Leonard was in the field but I'd take down the information.

"Pull up a chair." I motioned to the chair at the corner of the office. It would be easier to talk at eye level. I jotted down notes as he told me about the project, and continued with small talk as if I were an old friend.

"Now all I need is your phone number." I wrote it down next to his name. "I suppose you're going to tell me you're related to Tom Selleck," I smiled and said in a teasing voice. He had introduced himself as Bob Selleck.

"Well... actually," he grinned and gave a little chuckle, "...I'm his brother."

"Oh." My face flushed, my eyebrow raised in surprise, as I fumbled for something intelligent to say. "Hmmmm. You don't look like him." *What a stupid thing to say,* I thought.

"No, we certainly don't look alike." His laugh assured me he didn't take offense. Tom Selleck was a hunk back in the '80s. I wanted to say, "but you're handsome too!" I resisted the urge to insert my foot deeper into my mouth. He grinned as we shook hands.

"Leonard will be calling you," I said.

Great things come to you when you open the door
and step out of your comfort zone.

∞ ∞ ∞

Hard Decisions

J ohn had constant swelling in his feet and legs. At the end of his shift, he'd come home, prop his feet up in a recliner and read for an hour or more before going to bed. Elevating his feet helped the circulation, easing the swelling. He'd been working his swing shift for a year when he scheduled his routine checkup.

"Your body can't handle working an eight-hour shift. You need to prop your feet up every few hours to keep the swelling down. You're not getting the proper blood circulation sitting in your chair that long."

John slumped in his chair, a pained, defeated expression on his face as he relayed the doctor's words to me. He tried to convince me, as well as himself, that he could handle it.

"I can keep my feet up during the day before going to work," he said. He thought that would be the answer since he worked a night shift. But the problem was in sitting in his chair eight hours straight, whether it was day time or evening.

"Is the job worth the risk to your health?" I asked him.

Poor circulation meant the risk of additional medical issues. He knew that. And he knew he had to follow the doctor's orders, and quit his job. My heart ached for John. Once again, another dream of his was being shattered. He dedicated two years to earning his degree. He met that goal and returned to the workforce, only to be told that wasn't feasible. He was faced with a tough, but obvious, decision.

John believed the man should be the breadwinner of the house. It was hard for him to accept that his wife worked outside the home while he stayed home, with social security disability being his form of income. He took on the household chores; doing the laundry, cleaning the house, and even cooked dinner, albeit sometimes resorting to microwave TV dinners, depending on his energy. He joked about being "Mr. Mom."

John tried to keep a positive attitude but I knew he hated taking on the role of homemaker. One evening he snapped at us.

"You think it's easy cleaning up after you guys? Try doing it from this chair!" He lifted himself out of his wheelchair, shifted to a kitchen chair, and motioned for one of the boys to sit in his wheelchair. "Now, go ahead and wash off the table." The lesson was clear. John's positive mood gradually became darker.

I coaxed him to go for a ride with me one day "to run an errand." I stopped at a suburban home.

"I'll be back in a few minutes. I need to see these people about a project we're working on." I came back to the car carrying a purebred black Labrador puppy in my arms. I handed her to John.

"I thought you might like something besides the house to take care of." The little ball of fur instantly snuggled into John's neck and shoulder. I hoped having a puppy to train and keep him company would cheer him up. Beginning that day, Sallee seldom left his side.

We grew concerned about the big city lifestyle for teenage boys — and I secretly grew concerned about John's depression. I sometimes wondered if my working closely with so many men, and seeing me happy in that position, may have made John feel threatened. If it did, he never mentioned it.

I talked with John about a possible move to rural Grants Pass, Oregon, near my parents. I thought the move would be good for the boys and I hoped having family close by would be good for John. My father's health was rapidly declining. He had been incapacitated for the past year, unable to get out of bed. My mother cared for him at home. He wanted no part of living in a nursing home.

John liked the idea and we decided to make the move. I cried behind closed doors. I loved my job and the people I worked with.

Decisions are the hardest thing to make, especially when it's between where you should be and where you want to be.

John and his dog, Sallee - 1989

∞∞∞

Adjusting to Change

"We found the perfect house for us." John's voice was filled with excitement. He and Larry made a trip to Grants Pass in search of a rental home while I spent time training my replacement. "It sits on a hill above Fish Hatchery Park with a beautiful view." I was familiar with the area, having grown up in Grants Pass.

"The house sounds great, as long as living that far out of town doesn't keep the boys from being able to participate in sports." I knew from experience the downfalls of country living. Chris and Duane excelled in their first year of little league baseball in Simi Valley. I wanted them to continue that opportunity.

"I'll be able to drive them." John assured me.

———

It was my last day of work. Shelley made reservations for a private room at our favorite fish restaurant where Leonard often took us for lunch. When I arrived with Leonard and all the guys, I managed to hold back the tears — for a short time. Our table was glamorously set with cloth napkins and crystal drinkware. A small individual table, placed in a nearby corner, was adorned with a white table cloth, a beautiful bouquet of multi-colored Chrysanthemums and half a dozen perfectly wrapped gift packages. I was unable to hold back the tears when I opened a delicate gold, heart-shaped necklace. One-half the necklace was laced with tiny diamonds. I went home and cried some more.

———

The large picture window in our Oregon home framed a stunning panoramic view of the valley below us. Sitting atop the hillside on 15 forested acres put us above the misty morning fog level. The steep gravel driveway was edged by oak, pine, and madrone trees. Deer, jackrabbits, and cottontails were a constant in our front yard. When we first moved in, we had a peacock that visited us regularly. Its shrill call, often sounding like a baby crying, cut through the early morning silence when it perched on our deck at 5 a.m. The spacious wooden deck, extending the front of the house, was perfect for soaking in the view. The boys would coast on their bicycles down Keen Road to Fish Hatchery Park to enjoy the popular swimming hole. They pushed their bikes back up the long, steep grade to return home. John and I made it a priority to support our boys' sports, shuttling them to, and attending, their football, baseball, and track events. Once the older boys got their drivers licenses, they helped with some of the shuttling duties. We loved the country life, the house, the view, and neither of us seemed to mind driving the eight miles to town.

I took advantage of Shelly's suggestion to file for unemployment benefits and stay home with the family awhile. But, the employment office required me to go to a certain amount of interviews. I spent a short time on unemployment when one employer insisted on hiring me after he interviewed me three times, as an office manager for an herb processing plant. My door opened into the warehouse, and butted against the brokering manager's office. My desk never saw a clean smooth surface, being continually covered with the herb dust that filtered through the door and windows. I've often wondered if that's where my allergies originated.

I could hear the broker through the thin wall and glass window, as he made his sales calls, one after the other. His foul language was atrocious. I wondered if they all spoke that way, or if maybe he lost some sales because of his language.

One morning that thin glass window nearly shattered as he slung his office door open. *CRASH!* It hit the wall as it flew open. Shouting every swear word, accompanied by F-bombs, he stormed into my office, his tantrum raging. Evidently a brokering sell didn't go the way he wanted. Like an upset child, he started kicking the file cabinet, then punching it with his fist. The swearing, kicking, and punching went on for several minutes.

"You need to calm down! You're going to give yourself a heart attack!" I was fed up with his language and his actions. My voice was sharp. He glanced my way and stomped his feet in rebellion, like a child being disobedient to his mother.

"My therapist told me not to hold things in. It's good for me to get it out." He whined.

"Well, if you don't stop, you're going to give *me* a heart attack! I've had enough of your tantrums!" This wasn't the first I'd witnessed with him. I didn't like this boss and I was ok with him knowing that at this point.

BANG! His fist hit the cabinet one more time. His office door slammed shut as he retreated to his office and pouted. He didn't come out until after I'd left for the day. I laughed and shook my head in disbelief when, several days later, I overheard his conversation with the warehouse foreman:

"I have to be careful around Esther. When she's mad, she has a look that could kill!"

One year after I'd begun working for that company, the corporate office decided to close the processing plant. The broker planned to work from his home and asked if I'd consider staying on with him, working part time.

"I'm sorry, I'm not interested. I think I'll start my own secretarial business." And that's what I did. I rented a small office space where I performed miscellaneous secretarial duties for individuals and small businesses. A law firm hired me to transcribe a deposition tape. Shortly after, they called and asked me to fill in for a vacationing secretary, ultimately hiring me to fill that position permanently.

———

I had hoped our move to Oregon would brighten John's days. He spoke to my father daily on the phone. There was still a strong bond between them. My parents lived in a small trailer house, inaccessible to a wheelchair, so John couldn't personally visit him. With Dad confined to his bed, their daily phone calls had to suffice. Other than shuttling the boys, John didn't have much to keep him occupied during the day. He took a few temporary, part time electronic jobs.

John might comment on his symptoms occasionally but I never heard him question why this injury happened to him. Migraines, swelling ankles and feet, nerve tingling in his arms, upset stomach and depression, were some of the daily spinal injury symptoms John endured. One day he told me,

"I feel pretty good today! The only thing bothering me is a headache." I couldn't help thinking that I seldom got sick or had headaches, but when I did, I whined about it.

Household chores became lower on John's priority list. He said the effort it took him to perform those tasks didn't appear to be appreciated by us. We tried not to take advantage of his willingness to do housekeeping chores but I think the underlying reason he stopped was the stigma of being Mr. Mom. In the '80s that wasn't a popular, or accepted, position like it is in today's society. His depression increased.

"When I was at home after my accident, I had school and the prospect of a job to look forward to. Now I just feel useless." John told me one evening.

My father passed away one month after we moved to Grants Pass. John helped my mother with details of the funeral arrangements. We held a reception at our home. He missed those daily phone calls. Three months later John's 19 year-old niece was killed in a car accident. John's drinking increased. He managed to consume a case of beer each day. His moods were a pendulum of unpredictability. He might be quiet, withdrawn and sullen, or antagonistic.

One day the boys were home, entertaining themselves in their bedrooms. I was in the living room.

KABOOM! A loud, explosive blast shook the house. I raced to the family room, the adrenaline pounding in my chest like a drum. John sat in his wheelchair, a dazed expression on his face. His hunting rifle lay across his lap. Sallee, his faithful labrador, trembled as she cowered in a nearby corner.

The 30-06 slug pierced the outside wall, just above the wood burning stove. Too close to Larry's bedroom wall for comfort. My entire body burned with fury.

"What the hell are you doing?" I screamed at him, uncontrollably. The boys came rushing from their rooms. I decided it wasn't safe for the boys and I to remain in the same house. I ushered them to the car and we left.

The next day I went back to the house with the intent to pick up some clothes. John was in the living room. His face was pale; dark circles were prominent around his eyes — obvious signs he had not slept during the night; his body appeared fatigued as he slumped in his chair.

"Good morning." His voice was quiet; somber. I opened my mouth to speak, then closed it again. There wasn't anything to say. It wasn't a good morning. He continued, "I called the VA hospital today — they said their rehab program has a waiting list, but when I explained the situation, they said they could admit me as an emergency case."

"Good!" My answer was curt, but I didn't know how else to respond. I was glad he made the call, but I was still furious at him, and scared.

"They said to be admitted, the spouse is required to stay in the relationship and attend one class a week." He didn't make eye contact. He sat motionless in his chair — waiting. I stood watching him for what seemed like minutes. His gaze stayed on his hands, clasped nervously in his lap. Tears trickled down my cheeks as I looked at this man who worked so hard in life, now sitting in a wheelchair, his body, his spirit, broken.

Chapter Nine

The Codependent

John admitted himself to the VA rehab unit. I was pleased that he was getting help, but I grumbled to myself about the inconvenience of taking a day off work as I drove the two-hour round trip to the Roseburg VA Hospital for my required class. I often wondered what effect our slammed doors, screaming voices, and violent actions would have on our sons. *Should I leave or should I stay?* crossed my mind with nearly every argument. I decided an absent father would have more of a negative effect than witnessing a tumultuous marriage.

I assumed the classes would teach us about the negative effects of alcohol, things I was well aware of. Surprisingly, they didn't talk much at all about the patient. To the instructor, we — the students in this class — were the patients.

"Symptoms of Codependency" — the overhead screen was titled. I was not familiar with codependency. As I read the list, I quickly sat at attention; my eyes glued on the screen. I couldn't believe what I was reading. I felt like a mirror had been placed in front of me.

Most of the symptoms listed were life-long traits of mine; feelings I'd grown up with: low self-esteem, difficulty communicating and speaking true feelings, beliefs, and needs; aiming to please people; giving up the self in the process of pleasing others; having no defenses against other people's thoughts and feelings; having trouble being emotionally close to someone in an intimate relationship; experiencing anxiety, fear, and other difficult emotions. The one I'd acquired during my marriage was making excuses or covering for another person.

I was guilty of every item on the list. I realized then why the class was mandatory, to make the codependent aware of these symptoms. With awareness, maybe they could be changed. But, these were life-long patterns of mine. *Could I really change?*

I sat on a hard wooden chair as I waited for the counselor. The drab office lacked color, so typical of government offices. Books lined the shelves along one wall. The small window allowed a trickle of dim light into the room. This was a one-on-one meeting, ending the group sessions. We would discuss John and his homecoming the following week, after six weeks of treatment. As the counselor settled into her chair, she spoke softly. She explained the path ahead of us and discussed his diagnoses.

"Yes, John is an alcoholic, but there is more he is dealing with," she said. "John is chronically depressed." I was aware of that. She went on to say, "He also appears to be dealing with post-traumatic stress disorder (PTSD), and with this recent event, an obvious nervous breakdown." I was shocked at the additional issues she discussed.

"Each medical condition can intensify the alcoholic's desire to drink, basically because of the stress of it all. And, likewise, when alcohol is consumed, it complicates each of the other conditions. It's a Catch 22," she said.

After our meeting, I sat quietly in my car. I was nervous about John coming home and the dynamics of our relationship. In a foggy daze, I repeated the counselor's words — "Nervous breakdown." I'd heard those words many years before, at the Salem hospital in 1973. As I thought about that incident, other scenes flashed through my mind. I felt nauseous. *How could I have not made the connection? Why wasn't it obvious at the time?* I don't know the answer to those questions. I cried, regained my composure, and drove home. Knowing John's sensitivity to the issues, I never shared with him the connections I'd made that day. It was all water under the bridge now. Why bring up past drama? And, we never discussed the counselor's conversation and his diagnoses either.

*And something inside me just... broke...That's
the only way I can describe it.*

∞ ∞ ∞

Making a Connection

More than 15 years earlier, in 1973, when gasoline rationing smothered John's Texaco station business, he went on a rampage, throwing furniture through the front window of our home. His diagnosis: a nervous breakdown.

As I looked back over our marriage, I pieced together other suspicious incidents:

In 1974, our ongoing marital problems led to our separation. He reacted by breaking furniture, and throwing it through the window.

In February 1978, John panicked at the time of my cesarean surgery. His reaction repeated itself.

And now, this incident with a rifle — which sent him to rehab — was diagnosed as a nervous breakdown. *Were each of the previous incidents also nervous breakdowns? Why did I not make a connection, until now?*

"He also shows signs of Post Traumatic Stress Disorder (PTSD)," she told me. Could that explain his reaction when I'd wake him from sleep? I learned early on to rouse him gently by calling his name, rather than touching him. If I even gently shook him, he would wake up swinging. When I asked him about it, he seemed genuinely perplexed by his own reactions, never able to explain his actions. I suspected his brief time in the military might have played a role, but he never seemed willing to discuss those experiences.

I knew alcoholism was an addiction, but like many others, never having an addiction myself, I had the mindset that if he really wanted to quit, he would. It wasn't until I felt a necessity to lose some weight that I discovered I did, in fact, have a form of addiction.

I'll eat it tonight and I'll start dieting tomorrow... or, *I'll quit the sweets tomorrow...* It was always tomorrow.

I realized the stronghold that sweets had over me. I no longer keep sweets that I'm fond of in my house. I used to keep a dish of candy for the boys and their friends on the living room bookshelf. It would always be filled with things they liked but things I knew I could resist, like chewy caramels that I didn't like being stuck in my teeth. I don't bake because I know, when I pull that pan of chocolate chip cookies from the oven, I'll eat nearly the entire first pan, with half a gallon of milk. Being aware that I'm addicted to sweets has not kept me from eating them, I just know that when I do, I will probably binge eat whatever irresistible sweet is within my reach. When I realized I couldn't resist the sweets, it opened my eyes, for the first time, to possibly a hint of the struggle that someone with an addiction to alcohol, cigarettes, food, or other form of addiction, might be like... an often-uncontrollable battle.

And now I was being told John had more than one form of demon he battles. It wasn't just fits of anger or alcohol... but something much deeper — he was also dealing with that demon we tend to call "mental health."

It always seems impossible until it's done.
Nelson Mandela

∞∞∞

Volunteer Work

J ohn and I didn't separate after his rehab. I attended the meetings required by the hospital and, with him now sober, I decided to stay in the marriage. I knew we had a lot of rebuilding to do. How we would do that, I wasn't sure. The marital bridge was torn and tattered. Years of violent arguments, and malicious words had worn that bridge down, leaving it in a frail state.

I worked full time for the law firm, the boys were in school and sports. It was imperative for John to find an interest that kept him busy during the day. Something that gave him a purpose. He read an article about the Handicap Awareness and Support League (HASL), a non-profit organization. He attended a meeting. HASL's mission was to improve the lives of the disabled. John immediately immersed himself in the volunteer work. He accepted the position as editor of the Community Connection newsletter, published monthly by the organization. I volunteered my time as secretary to the organization. We purchased a house at the edge of town. This eased the transportation since I could often make it home in time to pick Chris or Duane up for baseball practice or games when John was out of town. Other times, Larry or Stephen, both with driver's licenses by this time, took turns transporting the younger boys.

It didn't take long for John's workaholic tendency to be in full swing. He served on more boards than I could keep track of. The advantage to the volunteer work, other than scheduled meetings, he could set his own hours. That allowed him to spend time reclining with his feet up. The volunteer work gave him a sense of accomplishment and pride. In addition to HASL, he was appointed to the Governor's Task Force for the Disabled, volunteered his time to accessibility surveys at city, county, and state parks. He served as secretary to the Oregon Paralyzed Veterans of America (OPVA). He made trips to the Portland/Salem area each month to attend OPVA's board meetings. Needing to keep his car in good running order for those trips, he took it to a shop to have some transmission work done. A desk clerk was calculating the cost.

"I've heard you guys charge an arm and a leg for this kind of work — would you be willing to accept two legs?" John tried to joke but his sense of humor often came across rather dry, and the desk clerk didn't see any humor in his question.

John convinced the City of Grants Pass to move all of its handicap parking spaces off the busy main street, to the corner of each intersection, making entering and exiting a vehicle safer. He participated in the Americans with Disabilities Act (ADA) and made the trip to Washington, D.C. with OPVA to present issues with accessibilities. July 26, 1990 President George H.W. Bush signed the first comprehensive civil rights law for people with disabilities.

Unless you are familiar with certain disabilities, it's easy to overlook amenities that have been placed to make life easier for the disabled. Curb cuts eliminate wheelchairs from having to hop the curb to get on the sidewalk; wider bathroom doors allow wheelchair access to a toilet; ramps (with the proper incline) make buildings accessible where steps eliminate them; wider parking spaces help a wheelchair user who needs his driver's door open to the max to get his/her wheelchair out of the vehicle. Before designated handicap parking spaces became mandatory, and handicap placards were issued, John had to park in a normal parking space.

"Will you move my truck for me so I can get in?" He handed

his keys to a stranger coming out of the store. A car had parked in the adjoining space. There was not enough room for a wheelchair to fit between the two vehicles. Certainly not enough room for his door to be opened wide enough to pull the wheelchair into the vehicle. To avoid that situation again, John resorted to straddling the line, taking up two parking spaces. It was his only assurance of being able to get into his truck. Occasionally he'd come out of the store to find a nasty note on his windshield. "You need to learn how to park!"

Before ADA laws, he couldn't use most restrooms in public places. The doors were not wide enough to fit a wheelchair. At a few restaurants we patronized, he entered through the back door and kitchen, unable to get up the steps at the front door. Waitresses would often look at him in his chair then turn to me and ask,

"What would he like to order?"

"I'm not sure. Why don't you just ask him?" I'd respond. In other instances, people talked louder as if his wheelchair meant his hearing was impaired. It was humiliating for him but he took it in stride. It fueled his determination to improve accessibility for the disabled. Most people are not deliberately being insensitive, it's because they lack the education, experience, or familiarity with accessibility issues.

I've overheard conversations where someone asked John about his injury level. I never heard him complain. What I would hear went something like this:

"My injury level should have made me a quadriplegic. I'm fortunate to be a paraplegic."

After John's rehab, I realized how much I blamed our arguments on alcohol. If he didn't drink, we wouldn't fight. It didn't take long to discover that alcohol was only part of our problem. We still had opposite personalities that conflicted. We still didn't communicate well. We still argued — not to the degree of screaming or throwing things; the arguments were less harsh but still existed. It seemed easy for us both to allow mole hills to become mountains. For those reasons, I welcomed — as I'm sure he did too — the trips out of town for his OPVA meetings. The three to four days away gave us a break from one another.

John's workaholic tendencies kept him busy but they didn't cure his headaches, his poor leg circulation, his aches and pains, nor did it curb his depression. He just dealt with those issues... as best he could. All his life he'd been susceptible to pneumonia and bronchitis. When respiratory issues added to his list of ailments, he saw the doctor. X-rays detected a spot on his lungs. He feared a lifetime of cigarette smoking had caught up with him.

It was February 1992, three years after John became sober, when we had another heated spat. This time John moved out. He found a small cottage one mile from our home. Two weeks after moving out, March 1, 1992, is when I received that devastating phone call from my sister, Mary.

After John's death, both Jim Harding, of OPVA, and Jan Trombley, of HASL, wrote tributes to John in their prospective newsletters.

Jim Harding, President of OPVA (Jim was also a wheelchair user), wrote in the June 1992 issue of the *Paralog,* (The Voice of Oregon PVA), titled: *"Reflection of a Friend... A Foundation of a New Era"*

"As I search for the proper phrases and thoughts to describe my feelings for John, I remember a statement one of the doctors uttered to me after a lengthy question and answer period following my accident. He looked me straight in the eye and said, — 'Jim, God has something for you to do, so you better be getting about the tasks He has for you.' — I believe John was about the tasks God had for him. If there is meaning to our existence, John, for me, exemplified the phrase — One person can make a difference. — John made a difference in my life. John's legacy is, 'No issue is too big, and one committed person makes a difference.' John's vision was an accessible outdoors for all of Oregon's citizens."

————

Jan Trombley, the first person I'd ever seen John become close with, served with him as a board member for HASL. She wrote the following about John in the March/April 1992 issue of the Community Connection newsletter, (of which John had been the editor) titled: "Saying Goodbye to John:"

"Some special people have an impact on lives when they aren't even aware of it. They make you laugh, cry, angry, thoughtful, reflective and stimulate your deductive processes. And usually are not conscious of the significance in others' lives. John Stark was just such a person. He could play the devil's advocate with ease, and just as easily join in your idea and embellish upon it and carry you to areas you weren't aware of. He could be your caring friend and hold deep concerns for others' wellbeing, and he could be your most stimulating advisor. Even when he purposely took on that role you held utmost respect for his far-reaching mind and analytical opinions."

The Josephine County Parks Department installed a plaque along the Rogue River at Chinook Park honoring John's work for improving the lives of the disabled. It is placed near the wheelchair path that leads to an accessible concrete fishing dock.

Life is a combination of hard times and good
times, happiness and sadness.

The Stark Family 1989
Larry, Stephen, me,
Duane, John, Chris

∞ ∞ ∞

Chapter Ten

Guilt and Grief

My grief manifested itself more in the form of guilt. It pointed its ugly finger, accusing: *you should have... why didn't you... if only you had.* Regrets, misconceptions, and shame were overwhelming. The newspaper reported: *Grants Pass man loses life after accidental gunshot wound.*

John had a fresh brewed pot of coffee, with a full cup sitting next to his chair. His computer displayed the articles he had been working on, while he waited for my sister Mary to arrive. He was cleaning his guns that day with the intent of selling them. Gun cleaning equipment surrounded his living room chair. He made phone calls, stating he was cleaning his guns, to me and to his mother that day. Regardless, I read suspicious in the eyes of people who offered their condolences. Days before receiving the death certificate, my oldest son, Larry, age 19, came in the dining room,

"Mom, we need to talk." We sat at the kitchen table. "You know the death certificate is going to say suicide."

"I know." I wiped the tears from my eyes, unable to say any more.

"We need to work together as a family on this." I suspected the worst and I presumed the boys did as well but until now, we hadn't discussed it with one another. I recalled the sheriff deputy's comment; the one that faded into a fog before he returned to his patrol car; the one I tried to push out of my mind; the one that prompted his checking on me.

"I spoke with your son the night of the accident. He said 'if it's suicide, you can't tell my mom, she'll blame herself'... Will you be ok?"

Constant replays of decision after decision made sure that I did blame myself. John once suggested, after smoothing over an argument, that the two of us go to the coast.

"It would be a waste of money." I said, dismissing the idea. "All we'd do is argue while we're there."

We basically lived payday to payday and a coastal trip would be expensive. I didn't want to "waste" the money. Everything the rehab counselor had said about making changes seemed to go out the window. Nothing really changed in our relationship except that John no longer drank. My feelings lay deep below a layer of calluses. I'd grown weary of making an effort at our relationship.

One evening, as the family busied themselves at home, John sat in his recliner. He silenced the TV and, with an expressionless face, his voice sounding sad and empty, he said,

"It's a strange feeling to be in a house full of people, yet feel so alone." I didn't understand the comment and didn't say anything in response. He turned the volume back up and continued to watch his program.

Why-didn't-I scenarios taunted me. I felt horrified and ashamed when another accusing thought popped into my head: *Well now you don't have to argue with him every day!* My battle took a physical toll, as well as a mental toll. After a 30-pound weight loss, my fair skin clung to my 111 pound, 5'5" skeletal structure.

To rid myself of the guilt, I had to let go of the fallacy of blame. I felt angered at his choice to take his life and not leave a note. I began to analyze the situation in a different light. Maybe my theory is right, maybe it's wrong. Regardless, the conclusion I made gave — what appeared to me — logical answers, and a small amount of closure to a painful chapter of my life.

John made a point of calling me and his mother, and mentioned "cleaning his guns." He'd made a fresh pot of coffee, one cup sitting next to him. He knew my sister would be coming to his house at a specific time. His computer was opened to the articles they would be working on. Unless John reacted on a spur-of-the-moment decision, which I doubt, these steps would point to only one conclusion: he wanted his death to look like an accident. An accident would be easier for the family to accept. But there was more that convinced me.

While in our thirties, John wanted to purchase a life insurance policy. I believed a life insurance policy, at our age, was premature. He wanted to protect his family in the event something happened to him. Ignoring my concern that it was a waste of money at our young age, he proceeded to purchase a $75,000 policy, with an accidental coverage of $150,000. How fortunate I am that he ignored my concerns at that time.

If John and I didn't reconcile after this recent spat, we would be in a dire financial situation, he knew that. If John left a note, his death would certainly be ruled suicide. Without a note his death could be ruled accidental. In that case, the insurance would pay double indemnity at $150,000 — enough money to pay off all of our debts and put some into savings. The death took place shortly before the arrival time of my sister, which meant she would find him, not his family. It all appeared to be carefully planned.

Due to the ruling of suicide, the insurer did not pay the double indemnity amount. They did pay the $75,000 since the policy had been issued in excess of 10 years prior to his death. And yes, it did pay off all our debts. It took a long time for me to shut out the little voice in my head any time I spent money received from the insurance company — the voice that whispered "John's life paid for this." Our marital problems may have been the straw that broke the camel's back, and I own up to my portion of the blame. If his end goal was to relieve his family of financial hardship — along with his own pain — he succeeded in that goal, and I cling to that solace. No matter the reason, his suicide left scars on all the family members.

No amount of guilt can change the past, and no amount of worry will change the future.

———

Research states the five stages of grief are denial, anger, bargaining, depression, and acceptance. I think I went through each stage in one form or another.

Denial is a defense mechanism that helps us protect ourselves from shock. Depression, also called preparatory grieving, can involve sadness, regret, fear, or uncertainty. It can also indicate that the person has started to accept the loss. Bargaining can involve desperation to try to prevent or deter the loss.

Although the stages are often discussed as if they happen in order, not everyone experiences them in the same way, and some people may get stuck in one stage longer than others.

These stages are a natural part of the process of healing and learning to live with loss.

Larry was right when he said we needed to deal with this as a family. It wasn't until years later, as I looked back at the way I processed my grief, I realized the boys were the ones who helped me through the loss, rather than me, as their mother, helping them. Larry married his high school sweetheart six months after John's death, at age 20. Stephen, at age 18, took over the handyman duties around the house for me, while he worked a full-time job. Chris and Duane, ages 15 and 14 filled their days with school, sports, and youth group activities. I was thankful for the mentors who stepped into their lives in the absence of a father, and in some ways, the emotional absence of their mother.

For the first 18 years of my life, I lived under my parents' roof. After high school, I spent a year living with my sister, either under her roof or nearby. But since then, John had been my rock, no matter how rough our marriage got. He was the decision maker, and I had grown accustomed to leaning on him when things didn't go as planned. But now, he was gone, and I was left to navigate the uncharted territory of independence. The weight of responsibility settled heavily on my shoulders as I realized I had to make my own decisions, without anyone to blame or rely on. The guilt and grief threatened to consume me, but after four long months of floundering through each day, I found a temporary fix. I slapped a band-aid on my wounds.

With Grief, first there is loss,
then comes the remaking of life.

∞ ∞ ∞

The Band-Aid

I wiped the sweat from my brow as I meandered out to the swimming pool area, my blue floral towel wrapped around my thin body. I paused to watch my 14-year-old son, Duane. He and his friend were splashing and dunking one another. Deciding not to get in the middle of a pool water fight, I chose to sit in a lounge chair shaded by an enormous colorful umbrella. I felt uncomfortable around so many people I didn't know. I distanced myself by going to the pool while others stayed inside, out of the sweltering July heat.

I became good friends with Jessica, Duane's best friend's mother. She invited me to a barbecue on the 4th of July, which was being held at her friend Carol's house. I accepted but as the date approached, my anxieties nearly caused me to change my mind. Jessica's family would be the only ones I knew.

The house bustled with people when Duane and I arrived. I immediately searched for Jessica. She introduced me to the hostess who gave me a tour of the huge beautiful home, specifically built for entertaining. Besides its large living space and gourmet kitchen, it had a recreation room with a billiard table and pinball machines. The fenced patio had a large swimming pool, and a sauna. The house was secluded in the woods a mile up the mountain, behind my house. Several large shops housed half a dozen classic cars in various stages of rebuild.

Most of the guests congregated in the air-conditioned recreation room. One of the guests cautiously approached me.

"Hi, I'm Mike. Do you remember me?"

"No, I'm sorry. Your face does look a little familiar."

He was wearing shorts and a tank top. In civilian clothes, I didn't recognize him as the officer who checked on me four months earlier. He asked how I was doing and we exchanged a few pleasant comments before he went on to mingle with others. I stayed close to Jessica and a few she introduced me to, feeling a little out of place. When conversation waned, I milled around the room checking out the amenities, then wandered out to the pool.

I smiled as I watched the boys having fun in the pool. I questioned myself, *is the smile a reaction to watching these two boys water fighting... or is it something else?* Across the pool from me stood a copper toned, shirtless body donning flowery swim trunks. He had thick dark, wavy hair. I chuckled at the quirkiness of his handlebar mustache. A flash of guilt hit me — why am I checking out this guy?

When the boys tired, they went inside. The tan body followed but not before exchanging a brief smile with me. In an effort to shake off the conflicting emotions, I eased myself into the cool, clear water. I had the pool to myself. I sat on the water-covered steps. I closed my eyes, listening to the sounds. Other than the faint, muffled laughter coming from the recreation room, the surrounding forest was silent, no rustling breeze to cool the three-digit temperatures. I sat alone, deep in my thoughts. Then I was startled by a voice above me.

"There you are." Jessica appeared carrying a glass of wine in each hand. She placed the wine on the table and joined me in the pool. "You OK?"

"I'm good. Just cooling off." I smiled. "Who's the guy with the quirky handlebar mustache?" I laughed, trying to get the focus off of me.

"He's Jim's best friend since high school." After a brief pause, her face lit up. "Come on, let me introduce you!"

"No, I was just curious. Maybe later." I fidgeted, face flushing now for even asking. She did introduce us later. I played several games of pool with Jessica, her husband, and their friend, Michael. We chatted in the sauna, played one on one basketball and I found myself enjoying the evening. The first time I'd really laughed in months. On the way home that evening, Duane teased,

"Gary asked me who the woman was that his dad was flirting with. When I looked to see, I told him, 'That's my mom!'" I glanced in his direction. Seeing the smile on his face, hearing the teasing in his voice, a sense of peace replaced the guilt for having fun. I thought, *It's alright, Esther.*

When Michael and I met, he was newly divorced, and I was recently widowed. I appreciated the little jolt of happiness I'd received in our relationship. I think it served as a healing band-aid for the two of us. He lived an hour away. We took turns commuting each weekend, for two years. We laughed at the similarities of our male-dominated households: I had four boys, he had three boys. His sense of humor kept me laughing. He enjoyed socializing and water sports. We took a week's vacation together, stopping in Reno, visiting Virginia City, hiking in the mountains between Tahoe and Sacramento, and visiting his parents in southern California. It was his birthday and, seeing a parasailing trip advertised, I purchased tickets. One for him to parasail, one for me to ride on the boat and watch. While Michael was in the air, the boaters tried to convince me to go.

"I don't like heights, and I didn't buy a ticket for me."

"You can pay the balance when we get back to land." they said. Eventually, they convinced me. When Michael was reeled back to the boat, I was strapped into the seat. The boat slowly moved forward, inflating the parachute. As the boat picked up speed, the cable lengthened, and the wind lifted me and the parachute into the air. I soared above the water at 180 feet. Then the boat slowed, and the parachute lowered me closer and closer to the water. They didn't reel me in. As my feet touched the water, the boat sped up, the parachute rose in the sky, and off we went again. All of a sudden, I began to feel a little nauseous. *I hope this ride is almost over*, I remember thinking. *The last thing I want to do is throw-up from 180 feet in the air!* I took slow, deep breaths of the fresh air trying to calm my stomach. I was reeled back to the boat without an embarrassing incident.

After two years of a long distance relationship, I began to wonder: *Are we wasting each other's time?* The relationship waxed and waned. Neither of us were willing to relocate our boys to another school. Seeing no future for us, I decided to remove the band-aid; we broke up. It didn't take long for me to regret my decision. We had so much fun together. I called him, wanting to get back together.

"You dumped me once. It's not gonna happen again."

I was devastated. I couldn't control my crying. I had no appetite. During our dating, I'd regained the weight I'd lost after John's death. Now that 30 pounds fell off once again, my ribs were visible under my skin. Every muscle in my body ached, and a weight bore heavy on my chest. I had no motivation to do anything. When at work, I struggled to stay focused. I was heartbroken and distraught. I felt guilty that a breakup of a relationship was affecting me as much, if not more, than my husband's death. *That just doesn't seem right!* I'd shared with my office manager, who was also a friend, about the difficulty of getting myself motivated to even show up for work.

One morning I continued to hit the snooze button over and over. That wasn't unusual. Not being a morning person, I always set my alarm 45 minutes before I needed to get up so that I could wake up slowly. But this morning, my body was refusing to get up. I knew it was time for me to leave for work but I hit the snooze one more time. I turned over and cuddled to my tear-dampened pillow. Before the next snooze cycle, the phone rang. I picked it up. It was my office manager, Sherry Watson.

"Good morning sweety, it's time to get up."

"But I don't want to!" I sobbed, sounding like a child not wanting to go to school.

"I know you don't, honey, but you can do this!" I made it to work, thanks to Sherry, albeit late. I knew I couldn't expect them to tolerate this behavior for long. As I left work that evening and headed to the alley where employees parked their cars, I had to pass Dr. Larson's office. He was a psychologist, with an office next door to the law firm. *You haven't been able to beat this yourself, Esther, maybe you need some help.* I walked in. With a tear-stained face, I made an appointment for the next day. I wasn't sure what he could help me with, but I didn't know what else to do. The first thing he did after listening to me babble my story was to prescribe an antidepressant, Paxil. I questioned him about it since so many warned me, "Don't be taking antidepressants" or other drugs. He explained that when the body's chemistry gets all out of whack, it has a difficult time readjusting. The medication would help. To keep me from being too groggy in the mornings, take half at night and half in the morning. It helped in the manner that I could think a little more clearly. He let me talk during the first few sessions, offering little to no recommendations. He jotted down notes. I asked him why I would be as devastated over a relationship breakup as I was with my husband's death. He finally broke his silence.

"I don't believe your grief is so much the loss of that relationship, Esther. I'm inclined to think your depression, in that area, is from a feeling of rejection. He no longer wanted you." That comment stung, but it had a ring of truth to it. I was feeling rejected, especially knowing he was already dating again. After recording most of my recent history, he suggested my depression had a much deeper root than heartbreak.

"From what I'm hearing, you've seen a number of deaths in recent years. It doesn't sound like you've allowed yourself to grieve over any of them. You've stuffed your grief. But, Esther, death isn't the only loss. You've had other losses too. You've stored up those feelings and the breakup was like a plug being pulled from the dam. Now, the grief is pouring out."

I thought about the doctor's analysis and recalled the events he mentioned:

———

"I think Les has had a stroke." It was October 24, 1987. My mother's frightened voice made me jump in the car and head to her house. My father was in bed, awake when I arrived. His face was pale and drawn. I picked up his hand. It felt cool and clammy to the touch. His eyes, previously looking toward the ceiling, moved to look at me. I wasn't sure if he was coherent or not.

"Dad, do you know who I am?" He slowly nodded yes, but couldn't speak. "Do you want me to take you to the hospital?"

He shook his head, ever so slightly, in a side-to-side motion, a frightened look in his eyes at the mere suggestion. He never wanted to be in a nursing home and he wanted to die in his own bed. It was a struggle for my small framed mother to care for him the past year but she did her best, and that seemed to be good enough for him. "Ok. We won't do that." I told him. The fear left his eyes. I held his hand as I talked with him, a one-sided conversation. When I got ready to leave, I kissed his forehead. As I turned away, I brushed my hand across my damp cheek, gave my mother a hug, then paused before going out the door, throwing him a kiss. "I love you." Those were my last words to my father. He passed away later that evening. At that moment, I was thankful I'd made the decision to leave a job I loved and move close to my parents. I had a month of quality time visiting with my dad, something I would have missed if we would have stayed in California. I buried my tears, trying to be strong.

A month before my father passed, my brother George stopped to visit Mom and Dad on his way to Texas. George told me of a conversation he had with our father as they talked about George going to Texas.

"I'm going on a trip soon, too." My father's voice was weak.

"Where are you going?" George asked.

"I'm going to see mama," my 84 year-old father said.

John helped my mother with the funeral arrangements. My father wanted to be buried next to his brother Merlin in a cemetery in Cave Junction. Though my eyes dampened a few times, I never broke down and cried. I told myself, *He's in a better place now.*

———

In January 1988, we got word that John's niece was killed in a car accident. She graduated from high school the prior Spring and was only a few years older than our son, Larry. The news was devastating to John --- he was still grieving the loss of my father. I snuck quietly into our bedroom, hidden from the rest of the family, where my tears flowed for several minutes — tears of heartache for Julie, her mother. After a few minutes, I dried my eyes, returned to the living room, and tried not to think about it again. The thought of any parent having to bury their child was unbearable.

———

In 1991, Dad Stark retired — he and Mom Stark bought a motorhome and headed for the Grand Canyon — they stopped to see us on the way. Mom snapped a photograph during that visit — Dad with his arm around my shoulders, both of us in a belly laugh. He and I had formed a close relationship from the minute we first met. A few weeks after that March 1991 visit, we received a call from John's sister, Julie. She and her husband, Dale, spent time with them in the Grand Canyon, then flew back home to Riverside, California. After deboarding the plane, they were immediately notified that dad suffered a heart attack while still at the Grand Canyon. He passed away prior to reaching the hospital. I couldn't believe he was gone. Once again, I held back my tears and stayed strong *for John's sake*, I told myself. I was in denial. To get through any grief of this loss, I'd push reality aside and tell myself, *I'll see him on our next trip to Washington.* Tears trickled down my cheeks at the memorial service. I wiped them away and didn't allow them to surface again.

John died 11 months after Dad Stark's passing.

———

"Sometimes death is easier to accept because it's final," my psychologist told me. He expanded on his answer to my previous question, "A breakup doesn't always have closure. In those cases, you still mourn the absence of the person who is gone."

He went on to explain the Empty Nest Syndrome: "Children grow up and leave home, creating a void in the household. That, too, is a loss," he said. "There's something missing from your life." My house was certainly feeling empty. A house once bustling with six of us, now saw me and Duane passing in and out. It all made sense. Larry married in September 1992, six months after John's death. My mother moved into Larry's room shortly after. In September 1994, she rented an apartment and moved out. Also in September 1994, Christopher left for college, and Stephen bought his first house and moved out. Duane and I crossed paths between school and work schedules. With all the changes in my household, the idea that Michael and I were wasting each other's time became more prominent and I removed that band-aid. The dam of emotions overflowed.

I knew now... it was time to focus on healing.

Sometimes healing requires
more time than bandages can offer.

∞ ∞ ∞

The Death Certificate

Understanding my psychologist's explanation gave me a little better perspective of my situation, but it didn't diminish the intensity of my grief. I didn't see what else he could do for me, so I canceled future appointments, and I stopped taking the Paxil. It was up to me to take control of my thoughts, rather than let them control me.

I was attending a time management seminar in Portland for my work but my mind kept wandering, unable to stay focused on the subject. Then through the fog of my brain something the speaker said caught my attention:

"Day in and day out, a river flows through the same channel. If you place a boulder in its path, the water will find ways to flow around it, cutting a new path. Eventually, that path becomes the main channel."

Since I had not been focused, I had no idea how that comment related to time management, but the comment stuck in my mind. I began to ponder its connection to my personal struggles.

I was still struggling with my grief. I wondered if the river's adaptability could be applied to my own life. *Why not give it a try?* As emotional storms brewed, I repeated the phrase like a mantra: *I don't need to think about this. — I don't need to think about this.* It became the boulder in my river of emotions. Some days, it seemed as if I repeated it thousands of times, but gradually the process worked. The darkness began to lift, and I saw glimmers of light. Instead of crashing every few days, I started to experience longer stretches of calm. I held onto hope that my candle would soon burn bright, and everything would be okay.

But, when the phone rang, the candle dimmed and the flame vanished, leaving me in darkness once again.

"Esther, I'm researching information that could mean grant money for the boys' schooling. Will you send me a copy of John's death certificate?" It was Mom Stark calling.

"I'll see if I can order one." I made a quick excuse to get off the phone. I grabbed the back of a kitchen chair to steady myself. My head was spinning and I felt nauseous. *How could I not realize this would happen some day?* I knew I would now have to face the consequences. It wasn't really a lie. I just didn't give them all the information. I never told John's family that his death was suicide. The death certificate would reveal that information. I called my brother-in-law, Dale Kort.

"Mom wants a copy of the death certificate." I broke down. "But there's a problem." Dale and I had become close over the years. His quirky, fun sense of humor made him easy to love. I could see why John's older sister, Julie, fell in love with this character. Dale listened as I awkwardly spilled my story, ashamed to keep such a secret, defensive about protecting John.

"I'll explain it all to Julie. We'll call Mom. You don't need to be the one to do that." Dale tried to calm me. I hung up the phone, relieved that Dale took the burden from my shoulders. It was several days later when the shrill ring cut through me like a knife. I knew it was the call I was dreading. I reluctantly lifted the receiver. Fighting back tears, I answered, low and quiet, trying to hide the tremble of my voice.

"Hello."

"Hello Esther. This is Mom." she paused. I opened my mouth but could only gasp, my heart pounding. "Julie and Dale called me." she paused again.

"I know you must be angry with me… for keeping that from you." I began to cry. Her voice stayed calm.

"Yes, I'm angry with you Esther, but not for the reason you think." She paused as if to collect her thoughts. "I'm angry that you bore the burden alone. You should have told us. We would have gotten through it together."

———

As I write this book, I received word that my precious brother-in-law, my confidant, my dear friend, Dale, has passed away. I visited him just days before his death. I stood next to his hospital bed which was placed in their living room. His wife, Julie, who took the most loving care of Dale throughout his declining health, stood at the head of his bed. I stood where I could see Dale's face and his sweet smile as we talked. I could tell he wasn't hearing much of the conversation Julie and I were having. Regardless, I stood where Dale could see me, wanting him to feel included in our conversation.

"You're enjoying looking at her, aren't you." Julie teased Dale, noticing his perpetual smile. In a soft meek voice, Dale answered.

"I'm just enjoying watching her talk." I will never forget those last hours spent with him, nor the many visits, and pleasure of knowing him for so many years. Rest in peace my dear friend.

*Anyone who has never made a mistake
has never tried anything .
Albert Einstein*

———

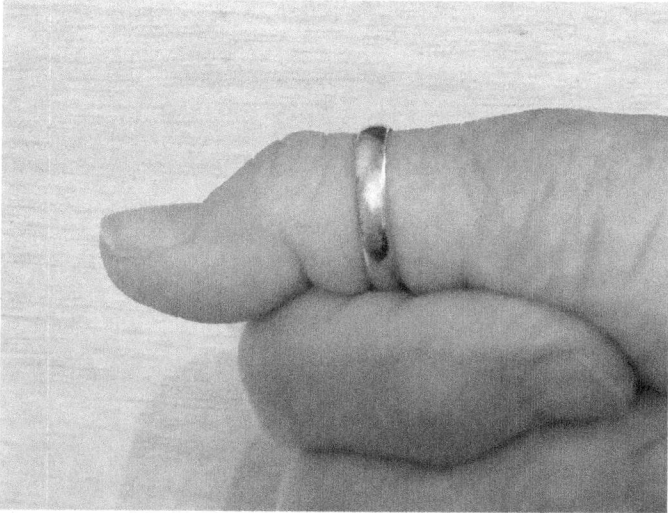

I continue to wear a gold wedding
band on my right thumb in honor of John.

∞ ∞ ∞

Part 2 – The Journey

Chapter Eleven

Psalms 37:4

I sought out verses in the Bible in an attempt to bring peace to my mind. The Psalms became my go-to book to study. I could relate to David's cries for the Lord to lift him out of the miry pit. I read the Psalms over and over. I kept coming back to Psalms 37:4 as if it had a special message for me. A message I didn't understand.

"Delight thyself in the Lord and he shall give you the desires of your heart."

What does that even mean? Like David, I cried out in frustration as I knelt in prayer next to my bed. I spent a lot of time on my knees in recent days. I knew there must be a meaning more than if I trusted the Lord, I'd get my wishes. *Dry your eyes and go to church, Esther.* The thought popped into my mind. I glanced at the clock. I could barely make out the time through the blur of my eyes. If I hurry, I'll make the Sunday evening service. I washed my face, and reluctantly obeyed the undesirable impulse that suggested I go to church.

I quietly slipped in the sanctuary door and sat along the back wall, where all the seats were empty. *I'll listen to the message and sneak out during the closing prayer.* I didn't want to talk with anyone, or answer questions about my bloodshot eyes. I was here only because my instincts – or the Holy Spirit – told me to be. The music ended and the pastor flipped through the pages of his Bible as he strode to the podium.

"I'd like you to turn your Bibles to Psalm 37:4." My brain fog quickly lifted and, like a puppy waiting for a treat, I sat at attention. "You're probably wondering what that means." *Yes! Yes, I do. Go on.* I felt impatient while he paused, waiting for everyone to turn to the page. "Like us, as fathers, God wants His children to curl up in His lap. He wants us to trust Him with our lives."

Trust. I realized I had not been trusting Him with a plan for my life. At that moment, I rededicated my heart. I prayed for strength to make the changes I needed to make in my life. The following week, I sent a letter to the pastor letting him know how God used him to answer my prayers.

Sometimes you don't need a plan. Sometimes you just need to breathe, trust, let go, and see what happens.

∞∞∞

Changing the Congo

I saw a quote by Donald Miller, author of Blue Like Jazz. He said, "Nothing is going to change in the Congo until you and I figure out what's wrong with the person in the mirror." I already knew what was wrong with the person in the mirror. What I didn't know was how to change her. That image reflected four decades riddled with crippling self doubt. I could go on surviving day after day, wishing I could live life beyond my fears, but what I really wanted was to shatter that reflection; stiffen the backbone; show some courage; and change the Congo. But how?

My shyness and fears interfered with every part of my life. I avoided taking risks because I was afraid of failure. I avoided expressing an opinion because I might be wrong or my opinion might not be the same as the person I was speaking with. I missed multiple opportunities because fear kept me from opening opportunity's door.

While cleaning the house one day, I picked up a piece of paper from the floor of my son's room. Before I tossed it in the trash, I looked to see if it was important. I read the words of a poem that went something like this: "I sit here looking outside. I'd like to join them but I don't know how. Instead, I sit here wishing, wishing, that I could be like them."

I cried. I knew the feeling all too well. That could very well have been me who wrote those words. A yearning to join in, to laugh and have fun; a yearning to be comfortable in groups; a yearning that I didn't know how to fulfill. I never told my son that I read that note, nor did I have a conversation with him about how to deal with his dilemma. Instead, my heart ached for him. I hadn't managed to overcome my own fears. I hadn't learned to live outside my bubble. How could I help him step out of his?

As I talked with my pre-teen grandson, the subject turned to girls. "I felt like a bump on a log, Grandma. I couldn't think of anything to say to her." A book lay on the table of a college student I visited. The title jumped out at me, *How to Overcome Anxiety*. I wanted to hug her, tell her everything will be alright. I didn't, because I didn't have the answer to fix things. In a crowded room I see a loner sitting at a table, busying their hands, avoiding eye contact, trying not to be noticed. I recognize those traits.

If I want to change the Congo, I have to educate myself. To do that, I'll have to read books on the process. I seldom read books. I'd lost interest in reading for pleasure during high school due to my difficulty staying focused. I'd read a page, then have to read it again. If I finished a book, after a period of time I'd remember the name but not the content... the same applied to movies. If someone asked me if I'd seen a particular movie, my answer would most likely be, "Yes, I remember the movie was good, but remind me what it was about."

I worried that my lack of comprehension might be genetic. My Grandpa George and Grandpa Stacy were brothers – my parents were cousins — making me a redneck, as comedians would call us country folk. They joked about cousins marrying cousins, which causes recessive genes. I feared there may be some truth to that. Maybe I was a redneck. Maybe I was less intelligent. I never publicized the fact my parents were cousins and I kept my comprehension issues a secret. I became a headline reader, scanning an article to get the gist of the content. If the article was too long, I'd quickly get bored and lose focus. Instead of books, I read magazines. The shorter articles were easier for me to finish — and remember. My lack of comprehension makes engaging in conversations awkward. I don't always remember enough details to contribute effectively, leaving me frustrated and feeling uneducated.

I knew I needed to overcome the fears in my life — and I needed to change the Congo, as Donald Miller wrote. As a step to make those changes, in spite of my secret comprehension problem — I ordered self-help books. *How to Make Friends and Influence People* – I hoped this would help me overcome my fear of socializing; *Speak Up* – one of my biggest fears that needed to be conquered; and *The 7 Ancient Keys to Happiness.* I'm not sure what I thought that last book would teach me, but it did prove to be of help at a later date.

Knowing I may not remember what I read, I underlined, highlighted and made notes in the margins. That made it easier to grasp the concept of the books. I still use this method when I read. My Bible is littered with notes in the margins, highlights and underscores, notes scribbled on the white pages inside the back cover. I reviewed the highlights of these new books over and over. At that time, the most valuable information came from the book *Speak Up.*

"When conversation begins to lull, ask people about themselves. People love to talk about themselves. As long as you ask questions about them, the conversation will continue."

Dale Carnegie's book *How to Win Friends and Influence People* also stated similar techniques:

"Talk to someone about themselves and they'll listen for hours. You can make more friends in two months by becoming interested in other people than you can in two years by trying to get other people interested in you."

I worked as a legal assistant at a law firm. Each of the assistants took turns making the daily courthouse run, which entailed a stop at the recorder's office.

"He doesn't say a word when I go over there," each assistant had the same complaint. "He never smiles, never attempts to make conversation." I thought about the book, *Speak Up*, as I walked to the courthouse one day. The recorder stood, came to the counter and reached for the documents – as usual, no smile, no hello. While he was recording, I noticed a picture on his desk. *Here's my opportunity.*

"I assume that's your son in the picture." I used my cheerful voice. He glanced at me. A smile crossed his face when he saw me pointing to the picture on his desk – a young boy holding a basketball.

"Yeah." I could hear the sound of pride in his voice.

"He's a cutie. How old is he?"

"He's 12."

I continued asking questions – "What position?" "What school?" He gave all the answers. I told him I had four sons. We talked about the sports they enjoyed. *Speak Up* broke the ice on that conversation, and it gave us a common link that was pursued for years to come. In my 26 years of working for the law firm, I watched his son grow up, graduate college, and get married — all vicariously through the stories he shared during my court runs.

If someone is quiet, it doesn't mean they are unsociable; they may be shy, like me. I try to make a habit of being the first to speak. Those first words of kindness may start a long-time friendship.

Reading is essential to those who seek to rise above the ordinary. - Jim Rohn

———

It wasn't until I was in my fifties that I finally shared my comprehension secret with the utmost trust of a close friend. I was shocked when he said he dealt with the exact issues. That gave me confidence to later share with another, and another. I learned that the lack of comprehension is a common reading disability. After five decades of hiding my shame, thinking there might be something genetically wrong with me, I discovered I don't have to be ashamed of the issue; I'm not a loner, as comprehension issues are quite common. I still wish I could fix it but I've come to realize, there are some things my brain does not grasp, and it's OK.

According to my best recollection, I don't remember.

∞ ∞ ∞

Meeting Tal

"Hi, I'm Tal." He offered his hand to shake. His dark wavy hair had a touch of gray above the ears. His smile appeared relaxed and natural. I liked that he made a simple introduction, rather than a cheesy pick-up line.

"Hello... I'm Esther." I shook his outstretched hand. He had a strong, leathery grip. I joined one of the Bible studies at church. When class was over, I made my way to the lobby, not lingering to meet anyone. That was a trait of mine. The lobby was where Tal Blankenship approached me. I recognized him from the class. When he'd introduced himself to the class as Tal, the instructor asked,

"Towel?"

"No, Tal, T-A-L."

"What did you think about the class?" Tal asked me, making friendly conversation.

"It was good." In all honesty, I had not found the class interesting.

"Yeah, a little dry, but good stuff," he said. After about 15 minutes of small talk (using my *Speak Up* technique) I found myself fidgeting. I shifted my notebook from one arm to the other.

"Well... I'm hungry. I'm gonna go home and fix a grilled cheese sandwich." I smiled awkwardly.

"That sounds good!"

"Want to join me?"

"Sure!" My invitation, as well as his response, shocked me. Tal followed me home that evening. I worried that, once we got to my house, I wouldn't know how to make conversation. You can only ask so many questions without it sounding like an interrogation.

I'd made a vow to myself not to get into another relationship until I'd fixed what was wrong in the Congo. Somehow, I'd need to clarify that with him. I didn't want to give false impressions with my invitation.

Tal carried the conversation as he sat on a bar stool at my kitchen island. I felt relieved he could make small talk with ease. I pulled out the cheese, bread, and my George Foreman grill. My nerves crawled across my skin as I tried to summon the courage to bring up the dating issue. Finally, I sighed in exasperation and nearly blurted the words.

"I'm not sure how to say this because it's kind of an awkward subject." A knot twisted in my stomach; the nerves continued to crawl. Tal waited; his eyebrow slightly raised in curiosity as if to say, "I'm listening." I drew in a deep breath, and continued, "I recently got out of a relationship and I've made a promise to myself that I'll spend time working on myself... and not get into a relationship again... for some time." My pause lasted the blink of an eye as my need to fill the silence kicked in. "I just didn't want to give false impressions with my invitation tonight."

"Thank you." Tal smiled; his expression relaxed. "I'm not looking for a relationship either, just friends." We both laughed as we sighed with relief. "I'm glad we got that subject behind us," he joked.

That invitation was the beginning of a lifelong friendship. Tal started teaching me ballroom dance, we watched movies together, and we bounced questions off one another. "I need a woman's perspective on something," he'd say when he called.

It was October 1995 when Tal invited me to a single's group Bible study, an extension of the Applegate Christian Fellowship he attended. I was hesitant to step out of my comfort zone, but I agreed. When the weekend arrived, I nearly changed my mind.

I immediately noticed Teri Mutz, who sat across the room from me. Her nervous fidgeting, the hesitant responses to direct questions, and the soft, quiet tone of her voice resonated deeply with me. Our shared awkwardness created a bond as we were drawn to each other. I was pleased to have someone I could relate to as we car-pooled to a single's retreat at the Oregon coast the following weekend.

The next major event for the single's group was Thanksgiving weekend. The church sponsored a community dinner and the singles group would be serving. Teri and I volunteered to take part. I enjoyed the opportunity to serve. I'd always pictured myself as someday volunteering with the Kiwanis, Rotary Club or other community organization, though I never opened the door to that opportunity. It didn't take long to realize I was among a group of vibrant and active people. After dinner was over, as we cleaned up, I made a bold move.

"I have leftover desserts at home, if you want to come over and help finish it off." I made the offer to a few people who served next to me. I held my breath in anticipation of a rejection. They probably have family parties to get home to.

"Sure!" Their response silenced the negative voice and I smiled. John and I never hosted events in our home. I began to feel nervous as I drove home. *Now what? How will I entertain them? — I'll deal with those questions when they arrive.*

I set out a stack of plates, silverware and leftover desserts. The doorbell rang and I welcomed my new friends in. I barely closed the door when the doorbell rang again, and again, and again.

"Is this where the singles are meeting tonight?" Over the next hour a total of 22 people showed up, bringing their leftover desserts. I discovered that an invitation to one of the singles meant an invitation to the entire group, unless specified otherwise. I didn't have to entertain them – they entertained themselves.

As I mingled with the crowd, I found myself listening more than contributing to the conversations. Yet, I felt a sense of pleasure and accomplishment as I observed the smiles, laughter, and chatter around me. I was pleased with myself for summoning the courage to extend the invitation, and grateful that I was welcomed with open arms as a newcomer into this energetic group.

Over the next year, my 1,400 sq. ft. house became a revolving door for activities of this 40's something group of singles. We gathered in the living and dining rooms for game nights; we played volleyball and badminton on the lawn; we swam and played water volleyball in the above-ground pool; a few relaxed in the hot tub or on the cedar deck for good conversation. The group mostly consisted of divorcees. A few never married. Me, the only widow. A common question I heard,

"How long have you been divorced?"

"I wasn't. I'm widowed."

"Oh, I'm sorry." Most people left it at that. The bold ones continued, "What happened?"

"He had a motor vehicle accident in '82 and broke his neck. He spent the last 10 years of his life in a wheelchair. The injuries eventually took a toll on his body." True facts - void of details. I had not learned to say "suicide." I'm not sure why I couldn't verbalize it. Maybe I thought it reflected on me as John's wife. Maybe I still carried the instinct to protect his good name. He was well known in the community for all the volunteer work he did, everyone respected him. *Would they think differently if they knew?*

Eventually, I got past the barrier of that ugly word. I learned to simply state, "It was suicide." I didn't elaborate. If they asked additional questions, I gave the same response but with an added phrase, "He had a motor vehicle accident in '82 and broke his neck. The injuries, *and depression,* eventually won the battle." As I allowed myself to say "suicide" — a sense of healing began to take place.

Word quickly spread through the group that I was not open to a dating relationship.

"We have a bet going on — to see who you'll date, once you decide you're ready," my friend, Jon, teased during a game night at my house.

"Why do I need to date? I have you guys to give me a hug when I need it." I laughed, then gave him a hug. As game night came to a close, he lingered behind.

"Thanks for letting us come over so often, Esther. We have so much fun here. Your house isn't just a house, it's a home! I can feel it." That comment stuck with me. I'd never thought of the difference between house and home. Now I did.

Years later, I saw a narrow wooden sign at a yard sale. It was a "must buy" for me. It brought back the memory of my friend's comment. The sign says: *A good home is made, not bought.* I proudly display it on my wall.

Confidence is not walking into a room thinking you're better than everyone. It's walking in not having to compare yourself to anyone at all. It is not "Will they like me" - it's -"I'll be fine if they don't."

Tal and his "boy" - Gus.

Chapter Twelve

An Empty Nest

During that year of interacting with my friends, my wounds healed — without the use of another band-aid. I found that my new friends appreciated me for my true self. I was still a quiet, reserved person, but I was learning to stretch my comfort zone, hiding some of my social fears. My fun came from providing a place for others to enjoy themselves. One night in church the pastor talked about spiritual gifts.

"I have no idea what my spiritual gift is," I told my friend Jack.

"I do," he responded immediately. "It's hospitality." I realized he was right. I've discovered that hospitality, and encouragement, are the things I do best.

Despite my love for entertaining in my home, I couldn't shake off the habit of comparing myself to others. I often found myself wishing I could exude the same level of confidence that others seemed to possess so effortlessly. The self-assurance they exhibited was a quality I struggled to embrace, leaving me feeling like I didn't quite measure up.

It was September of 1996. Duane was the last of the boys to move out when he started college. He moved to the dorm at Western Oregon University in Monmouth, Oregon, four hours away from me. I stood in Duane's bedroom doorway. A room void of his personal belongings; a vacuumed carpet now visible, an unusual sight.

When John and I bought this house in 1989, the boys got their own bedrooms — a first for them. At that time, I gave them a new household rule:

"From now on, you do your own laundry. When it's dry, take it back to your bedroom." Even Duane, a fourth grader, was old enough to learn the task, I thought. Since I was a full-time working mom, this eliminated one more household chore for me, and eliminated the clean clothes from being piled on the sofa for several days while everyone picked through it, pulling out one item at a time. Whether they made it to their dresser or closet would now be up to them. In Duane's case, they usually made it to one end of his bedroom floor. Seeing his floor covered with clothes one day, I felt frustrated.

"Duane, you need to get all these clothes off the floor and washed."

"But half of them are clean."

"How do you know what's clean or what's dirty? They're all over your floor."

"That side is clean and this side is dirty." To me, the dividing line was invisible.

Now, in 1996, I moved slowly through the house, tears trickling down my cheeks, overcome by nostalgia, as I reflected on the new chapters in each of the boys' lives:

I missed the one or two nights a week I had with my grandson, Jacob, while his parents attended night classes at Rogue Community College. They had recently moved to Corvallis where Larry, and his wife, Shantel, began attending Oregon State University full time. *— At least Duane will be living close to them,* I thought. Western State University is a half hour drive from Corvallis.

Larry's room was now vacant of both his belongings, and my mother's belongings, who used his room later. Those bedroom walls, once covered with Larry's baseball and football posters, were bare. I imagined the shelves looking as they once did, filled with binders, stuffed with baseball cards. I could almost hear them calling out, "Larry, Larry." That was something Larry would say if we were out of town for a weekend and he was anxious to get back to his baseball collection. "I can hear them calling my name," he'd say.

Stephen's room was always orderly. He had a place for everything, and everything was in its place. He chose to work a job rather than spend countless hours at sport practices. He bought his first house at the age of 21. His home was only a few miles from mine but I no longer had the pleasure of seeing him come in and out each day. His bedroom at my house was empty.

Christopher's room was a showcase of electronics when he lived at home. At age 15, he completely rebuilt the motherboard in our computer. Before leaving home to attend ITT Technical Institute in Portland, he removed the flashing lights, speakers, and wires from his sound system that stretched across his room, and all his computer equipment. I missed the essence of his electronic clutter.

Little by little, the house had gotten quieter as each fledgling set out on his own. Each bedroom, now clean and neat, lacked what made my house a home. I was left alone, with my cat, Mischief. My heart ached. I filled the void with group activities — trying to drown out the suffocating silence. When the crowds left, I faced the unsettling stillness of an empty house. I became restless. I needed more but I wasn't sure what I needed more of. Then I recalled something from my past: At the time we decided to move from southern California, the thought had crossed my mind — *if I was ever single, this is where I'd want to live. — Well, here I am, single. Is that what all this restlessness is about?* I wondered. I went to the river — my solace in times when I needed to clear my head.

Clumps of damp grass covered the lawn at Riverside Park, evidence the maintenance crew had arrived earlier. I placed my nylon poncho liner on the sloped bank, overlooking the Rogue River. As I stretched my body across the blanket, I closed my eyes. I listened to the nearby sounds; the rhythmic slapping of water against the river bank; the rustling of the crisp, dry leaves as the breeze scattered the multi-colors to the ground; the giggles of children as they fed the panhandling ducks and geese; and a songbird who serenaded me with a beautiful melody, from a nearby tree. When the singing stopped, I opened my eyes to see the bird take flight, leaving behind the stage from which he'd been performing. The clouds caught my attention. They evolved from one shape to another, quickly moving across the sky. *Change is inevitable,* I thought. *Maybe I do need a change.* A gust of wind swirled the yellow and gold leaves around me. An osprey's whistle announced its arrival as it circled its nest, ready to land.

"Thank you," I whispered, facing the Heavens. I stood, shook the damp grass from my blanket and folded it up. *I think I have my answer.* I spent the next few days contemplating the reality of such a decision. *It will be tough, but I'm going to do it.*

YOU WERE SHY?

Every positive change in your life begins with a clear, unequivocal decision that you are going to either do something, or stop doing something.

∞∞∞

175

One, Two, Three, Jump!

I was familiar with the expression, "Look before you leap." I'd been thinking about this idea off and on. Now I'd given serious thought to the idea for several days and I was ready to jump.

"Got a minute?" I asked as I stood in the doorway. I glanced at the piles of papers and files in disarray on his desk, smiling as a memory popped into my head. While my boss vacationed one year, I weeded through the stack of outdated magazines on his desk, returned many files back to mine for further work, straightened the books and papers, and tried giving some form of organization to his office. I never attempted that again. For weeks after returning from his vacation he'd ask me, "Do you know where…. is?" I discovered he had some idea of the content of his unorganized mess. He could work with the clutter. I, in contrast, found it necessary to tidy up my desk every night before leaving the office.

"Sure." Richard Adams never hesitated to give me his undivided attention when I needed it. I closed the door as I entered. A look of concern crossed his face. A closed door spells private.

"You know Duane left for college a few months ago." He nodded. I paused to calm my nervousness. "I loved southern California when John and I lived there. I've always had a desire to go back. Now, with the boys gone, I have no kids at home to keep me here; I have no man to keep me here," I said, laughing. "It's time to give it a try. I'm going to move to San Diego."

His wide eyes stayed fixed on me, waiting as if there would be a punchline. I'd been his legal assistant for eight years. He'd trained me. Though he practiced most areas of law, workers compensation and personal injury cases were his specialties. I took pride in my skills as a legal assistant; he'd trained me well. I couldn't ask for a better boss. But I needed to settle the restlessness that seemed to consume me the past few months.

"I'll be leaving at the end of the year." I gave him four months' notice. There were a few people who thought I must be crazy to give that much notice, saying he would certainly let me go as soon as he found a replacement. I didn't have that concern. I admired this man and held him in high esteem. I'd started with the firm doing word processing for several attorneys. During a reorganization of the office, he had requested to train me as his legal assistant. We developed a professional bond built on mutual trust and respect. I wanted to be sure he had time to find just the right person. Then, surely, he'd want me to train her. That would take time. Four months should be sufficient. A month passed. Richard had not posted an ad for help. Two months passed.

"When do you plan to hire someone?" I was concerned about ample time to train.

"I've been thinking about it, Esther. I'm not going to hire anyone." He paused, watching my eyebrows raise in question. "I'm going to do as much work as I can, myself. I'll spread some of the work out to the other secretaries. I think you'll be back. You're not going to like it down there. I'll see if I can get by without hiring someone... for now."

Astonished at his faith in my return, I worked at tying up as many loose ends as possible before my departure. My last day of work was December 31, 1996. I spent the month of January 1997 sorting a household of 13 years' accumulation. Any items the boys were interested in went in their direction. I kept only the things I would use. January was too cold for a yard sale, so I arranged for a non-profit organization to pick up a full truck-load of miscellaneous items. I hadn't applied for any jobs in San Diego yet. I'd do that in February, after Rosita's wedding, in which I'd committed to being a bridesmaid.

I arranged to spend a week with Julie and Dale, in Escondido, while job hunting. When I headed south, I spent an enjoyable three days with Leonard and Shelley Liston, my former engineering boss, and his wife. It had been 10 years since I'd left his company. We stayed in touch with annual Christmas letters. After I arrived at Julie and Dale's, I scoured classifieds, sent out resumes, and attended several interviews. San Diego was a 45-minute drive from Escondido. By week's end, I had a job offer at the corporate office of a large construction company in La Jolla, 12 miles north of San Diego.

"I have one crazy request. If I accept the job, can we push the start date out to March 1st? I'm supposed to be in a wedding late February. I need to find a place to live and get moved down here." I was surprised at my boldness to ask and delighted that they were impressed enough with me to hold the job position open for another month. I prepared for my next step: find a place to live.

Stephen and his fiancé, René, helped load my belongings in a U-Haul truck. Stephen drove the truck, and they pulled a dolly with René's car in tow so they had transportation back home. I drove my car. Each item I'd kept fit perfectly in the two-bedroom condo I rented for me, and Mischief. I looked forward to this new chapter in my life, sunny skies, and the condo's amenities; a fitness center, swimming pool, and hot tub.

March 1, 1997, I started my new job. There was little training for my position. I struggled through the process of learning California's construction law on my own. California has a 10-

year statute of limitations for construction defects. As 10 years approached on a dwelling, owners would file lawsuits for any items they suspected might have defects. In doing so, every contractor who worked on the building got pulled into the lawsuit. My job was monitoring those lawsuits, until it was determined that no defect was found within the scope of our contracted work. Monitoring construction law turned out to be a dry and unfulfilling experience, consisting of endless paperwork and no client interaction. I quickly got bored sitting behind a desk for eight hours.

In the first few months, I made two trips back to Oregon; the first to attend Stephen and René's wedding on April 26th, and a second trip a month later to meet my adorable second grandchild, Mikayla, born to Larry and Shantel on May 4th.

The warm San Diego weather was captivating, but my job was a major letdown — as was the social life. The workplace lacked any form of personal touch, laughter, or joy. The atmosphere was always somber and quiet. I tried to make friends with one gal and invited her to go rollerblading at a small lake not far from my condo. She also attended a Buddy Holly tribute concert with me. Finding we had very little in common to discuss, I stopped the invitations.

San Diego's environment didn't make it easy to meet new people. Unlike my rural upbringing, where greeting others with a friendly "hello" was a common courtesy, San Diegans seemed hesitant to engage. When I attempted to greet strangers with a smile and a hello, I often received scowls or was deliberately ignored, as if striking up a conversation with a stranger was frowned upon.

I became frustrated after five months of working at a dull job, and not feeling any connection with co-workers. I decided to start looking for another job in the area.

It was mid-July. My former boss's birthday arrived. I emailed Richard to wish him a Happy Birthday, and he surprised me with a call.

"Are you ever coming back home? I really need to hire someone." Though I was contemplating a new job search, I hadn't entertained the idea of returning to Oregon yet.

"Can I think about it for a day or two?" I didn't want to make a spur of the moment decision. My intentions were to adjust to the big city life, make new friends, and interact with them as I'd learned to do in Oregon — reevaluating the situation in one year. It had only been six months since I left the law firm. *I haven't accomplished my goal yet... or have I? What exactly was my goal in moving south?*

I considered his offer over the next few days — gaining a new perspective on my desires and goals. I realized that the timing of my move to, or from, Oregon wasn't the issue. What was important, was the fact that I trusted myself to take the leap, uproot my life, find a job, and start fresh in a new city. I acted with confidence in my ability to make it work. The job and social life in San Diego was not as glorious as I'd envisioned, but I'd taken the risk — and I discovered I could do it on my own. Richard's willingness to hold my position open for six months, with the offer to return with the same benefits and seniority as when I left, was a testament to my capabilities. His vote of confidence meant a lot to me. I did return to Grants Pass and my job at the law firm. Larry and Stephen flew to San Diego, loaded a U-Haul truck, and helped with the driving back to Oregon. Once back at the law firm, I continued working with Richard Adams for another 18 years.

Within a month of returning to Grants Pass, I received a call from Shelley Liston. Leonard had an opening at the engineering firm. He hoped I'd be interested in leaving San Diego to come work for him. Had I not already returned to Oregon, I'd have snatched that job up in an instant. The offer to return to the engineering firm, over 10 years after I left that job, spoke volumes to me — confirmation that they valued me and my work ethics. But now, I knew I belonged in Oregon.

There's no place like home!

Twenty-three years later I learned that Leonard lost his battle with cancer. I admired this dedicated family man and his business ethics. I gained a sense of belonging when I worked for his engineering firm. His willingness to rehire me 10 years after I'd left his firm did amazing things for my self-esteem. I'll forever feel gratitude for this incredible man.

You never know what you're capable of doing,
until you take the risk of trying.

∞∞∞

Getting Re-established

"**N**ow that you're back, do you think you and Tal will get together?" Within a two-week period of returning to Oregon, a half dozen people asked me that same question.

"Why would things be any different?" I shrugged my shoulders. I missed Tal while I lived in San Diego, but while I was there, I'd still get that occasional call, asking for a woman's opinion. We were still best of friends.

I immediately immersed myself back into the social activities I'd left behind. Teri met a guy while I was in San Diego and they eventually married. A friend introduced me to Sharon Canfield after an evening worship service. She was tall, slender, pretty, and I could tell, slightly shy. The second time we met, we were carpooling to hike a trail at Babyfoot Lake. Our conversation led us to our work. We discovered we were employed in competing fields — she, a workers compensation insurance adjuster, me working for the claimant's attorney, defending workers comp claims.   Our personalities immediately connected. Weekends soon became filled with group activities of hiking, snow skiing, and rafting. A large group of us signed up for ballroom dance lessons, at Tal's persuasion. We progressed through each eight-week session, reaching the final advanced class. We continued game nights, potlucks and listening to live music at the Solid Rock Cafe after Friday night worship services. I'd order a hot frothy vanilla steamer (milk), while others sipped their espresso coffees. No matter how hard I tried, I was never able to learn to like the taste of coffee.

Sharon and I spent many hot, summer Saturdays floating the

Granny Run section of the Rogue River. My sister and I named the five-mile stretch of river the *Granny Run*, due to its lazy water flow. Sharon and I hooked our inflatable kayaks — also known as Tahitis — together with bungee cords, stretched our bodies out, and sunbathed as we spent the next three or four hours chit-chatting our way down the river. The beauty of the river and its surroundings was never disappointing — and neither were our girl chats.

The bond Sharon and I established in 1997 stands strong. As of the writing of this book in 2024, we are backdoor neighbors.

> *Go confidently in the direction of your dreams.*
> *Live the life you've imagined.*
> *Henry David Thoreau*

∞ ∞ ∞

Sharon and me going
to a ballroom dance.
1999

Sharon and me. Still best friends - 2021

∞ ∞ ∞

Chapter Thirteen

Conquering
the Marshmallow

I cautiously carved a path through the snow, making my way down the steep hillside. By the time I reached the bottom of Marshmallow, my green snowsuit was covered in icy white powder. I kept track — I'd fallen 22 times.

We had a group of 13 who rented a large house for the weekend in Sun River, a ski resort town. Only David, me and two other guys snow skied. The others explored the tourist areas of town.

I'd only skied once before, when I went with my son and his friends. On that family trip, I had no idea how to ski, but I tried. When I fell, I couldn't get back up. I stayed in a crouched position, rode the bunny hill to the bottom, took off the skis in frustration, and sulked next to the fireplace for the remainder of the day. I was embarrassed that five-year-olds could fly past me on their skis while I struggled to get off the snow-packed ground. I wasn't going to face that situation on a second try.

This time will be different. I decided to take a quick lesson before attempting Mt. Bachelor's bunny hill. The short lesson taught me what I needed to know most, how to get up after falling.

My friend, David Jack, faithfully stayed with me rather than skiing with the guys. After a dozen trips down the bunny hill, falling and getting up, falling and getting up, I decided I was ready to ride the lift to the next level, the Marshmallow.

We stood in line for the ski lift up Marshmallow. I smiled — for David's sake — while inside I wanted to turn around and head back to the bunny hill. *I can do this. I can do this.* I repeated over and over to myself. I felt like the little train in my childhood books... "I think I can, I think I can, I know I can, I know I can." Before I could back out, the lift scooped us up and we were on our way to the top of the next level ski run.

"Gently push yourself off the chair, paying attention to your balance," David told me. "You'll do just fine."

My heart pounded as we neared the top, I prepared to push off. David hopped off first, I delayed. Then in a panic I jumped. The lift operator at the top reached out to grab one of my arms, trying to steady me. My skis hit the ground and kept going, not waiting for my body to catch up. I fell to the ground, taking the lift operator with me. David rushed to my rescue and, along with the lift operator, helped me back to my feet. At that moment, I was sure I'd never attempt skiing again! But David encouraged me and patiently stayed close as we skied down Marshmallow. When we reached the bottom, I'd fallen enough, without injury, to move me past my fear.

"You can go join the other guys now, David. I've got this."

I made several more trips down Marshmallow that afternoon — alone — with fewer falls each time.

Another time I went to Mt. Bachelor with Stephen, René, and our friend, Don Sutherland. Stephen and René boarded the lift ahead of me and Don. The two of us got in line and waited our turn for the lift to come around. I heard the lift arriving behind us. I turned to look at it and realized I was not lined up with the seat. At that moment, too late for me to shift my position, the lift collided with my body, knocking me into the small ditch. The lift operator stopped the lift, helped me out of the ditch and into the lift chair. I buried my humiliation, laughed about it with Don, Stephen, and René, and continued to enjoy the day. While the four of us were on a later lift, halfway up the mountain the lift came to a stop.

"Where's Mom?" Stephen immediately looked around.

"It wasn't me this time!" I was safely seated in the chair lift behind them.

———

I cherished the time I spent with my friends, but when it came to longer vacation times, friends and family had their own busy schedules. It was impractical to always coordinate my vacation time with them. It was time to be brave, and take the next step.

Gaining confidence is a journey.
It doesn't happen overnight.

ESTHER STARK

Me skiing on the Marshmallow slope.

∞ ∞ ∞

Staycation or Vacation

he *7 Ancient Ways to Happiness* book sat on my shelf for a number of years before I opened its cover. Paragraphs soon became highlighted, asterisks in the margins, and sentences were underlined as well as highlighted if they warranted special attention.

"If your dreams feel out of reach, break them down into smaller steps. If you want to travel but it seems out of your budget, take day trips, or weekend trips," the author wrote.

I didn't like doing things alone. I had friends tell me they eat out, or go to movies, alone. But not me — at least not yet. I tried to pump up my courage. *I can do this*, I told myself. I convinced myself to go to a movie alone, to see what it's like. It was a tear-jerker chick-flick titled, *Stepmom.* There was another couple in the theater, no one else. They sat several rows behind, and across from me. The woman loudly sniffled and blew her nose throughout the entire movie. The only advantage to attending that movie alone was that I could silently wipe my tears without anyone noticing. I decided I wouldn't attempt that again.

After studying the *7 Ancient Ways to Happiness* book, I convinced myself that I could vacation alone. If I didn't make that choice, all my vacations would end up as staycations. I decided on a plan. When vacation time arrived, my 1997 Ranger pickup — I'd purchased it brand new in San Diego — was hooked up to my stand-up jet ski trailer. The bed of the pick-up held my bicycle and my yellow molded plastic, sit-on-top kayak. For me, time off work wouldn't feel like a vacation if it didn't include a body of water nearby. As I drove the three hours, crossing the Siskiyou Mountains, I began to second-guess my vacation decision. *Will I have any fun doing this alone?* I reserved a week at an inexpensive motel with a pool, in Redding, California. The week's temperatures were predicted to reach 110 degrees. I liked the warmer temperatures if I planned to be on the water.

Reluctant, but determined, this week I would drag myself out of bed at 6:30 each morning. I'm a night owl but I needed to be an early riser to beat the scorching heat. I'm not a breakfast eater so a cup of microwaved Swiss Miss hot chocolate would suffice in the early morning hours. Breakfast, while growing up, was a cup of hot chocolate and a piece of toast before catching a bus to school. I've kept that routine, minus the piece of toast and bus ride. I never got up early enough to eat breakfast before going to work.

After arriving in Redding, I checked out the trailhead of a popular bike path I'd read about. My plan was to ride each morning before temperatures rose too high. In the afternoons, I'd spend time on the water. After downing my morning cup of hot chocolate, I slipped into my biking shorts and a tank top; filled my water bottle; and tucked a neckerchief in my backpack. If I got too warm on the ride, I could douse the neckerchief with water to help keep me cool. After grabbing my helmet and sunglasses, I was off for my first solo vacation adventure.

The bike path was a five-mile loop that hugged the Sacramento River. Solid-packed dirt made it an easy ride, and it offered gorgeous views and a serene atmosphere. Towering trees provided a welcomed respite of shade from the early morning sun. I navigated the obstacle course of Pine cones scattered about the path. Playful squirrels ran through the shrubs and onto the road. One fearless little critter raced alongside me, ultimately daring my braking skills as he darted across the road in front of me. I reacted quickly and, though my bicycle wobbled uncontrollably for a few seconds, I managed to stay upright and continued on my way.

The early morning rides put me back to my room by lunch time. I pulled the mayo and mustard from my cooler, slathered it on sourdough bread and topped it with thin sliced, oven-roasted turkey, and a sliver of red onion. Placing the prepared sandwich on a paper plate, I'd grab a plastic red solo cup, fill it with ice cubes, then pour a can of chilled Pepsi over the top — a little at a time as I waited for the frothy carbonation to settle down. In spite of the heat, I'd eat my lunch in the shade of a large, red-and-white striped umbrella, next to the pool. That was my lunch routine every other day. On rotating days, I'd make a quick trip to Burger King's drive-thru for a Whopper Jr meal — extra salt packets to go please. Dinners consisted of a chicken sandwich at McDonalds, or an order of extra-crispy Kentucky Fried Chicken with mashed potatoes. One night I went to Applebee's — and sat inside — alone. I didn't like the idea but it was on my list of comfort-zone challenges. I took a magazine to read while I waited for, and ate, my meal. I didn't make eye contact with other customers — only the waitress who took my order. The afternoons involved water sports but always ended with a relaxing evening, on a floaty in the crystal clear, cool, water of the pool.

The Sacramento River, California's largest river, is an important source of water to northern California's agricultural communities. It also provides refuge to various birds including bald eagles and migratory songbirds on stopover flights. Its relatively shallow, slow-flowing water provides the ideal setting for a solo kayaker. I dropped the tailgate down on my teal-green truck — the perfect color for a girl's truck — and pulled out my yellow sea kayak, my double bladed paddle and slipped my arms into my life jacket. As I waded into the slow current, the water rippled around my ankles, splashing my calves with cool water. The soft soil squished between my toes, muddying the water and stirring up a smell of wet earth and fish.

Pushing my kayak into thigh deep water, I placed my bottom in first and swung my legs over the side, catching my balance as the watercraft rocked. I dug the paddle into the water, thrust it to the rear of the kayak, and rotated the thrust from side to side, making my way upstream. I stayed as near the shore as possible, eliminating the stronger current. Even a slow flowing river provides a good workout of the arms and abdomen. I paddled and paddled. If I stopped, I'd lose ground as the current carried me back several strokes. *Don't rest, just paddle.*

I paddled as long and as hard as I could — until my arms screamed, *enough already!* I knew the float downstream would be fast. I wanted the ride to last as long as possible. I pulled my paddle into the kayak alongside me and lowered the back of my seat to a near zero incline. With my rolled towel placed under my neck, I stretched my legs out and closed my eyes. The river did the rest, carrying me back to my launch destination.

The following day was blazing hot. Too hot for any kind of physical exercise. I spent the afternoon at Whiskeytown Lake. I made several runs across the lake. The zigzag motion sent a spray of water over the front of the ski, cooling my body. Refreshingly drenched by the cool lake water, I headed to the shore, and my blanket. I slowly motored in. A teenaged boy, probably 15 or 16, stood on the bank watching. I pulled the ski onto the bank. No need for an anchor.

"That looks like so much fun! Are they hard to drive?" he inquired, admiring my small Kawasaki, stand-up jet ski. I recognized the envy in his eyes. It brought back a memory of my son, Stephen, when he was 13 years-old. John and I had taken our family on a weekend campout with my engineer coworkers when we lived in Simi Valley, California. One of the guys brought his stand-up jet ski. Seeing the envy in Stephen's eyes, David gave him a lesson and let him ride. That's all it took to spark Stephen's passion for water sports. I couldn't offer any less for this young teen. I paid it forward.

"Would you like to give it a try?" I asked.

"Are you kidding?" His voice hit a soprano note.

"Ask your parents, then let's go!"

Unable to contain his excitement, he ran like a child, hollering to his parents, who gave their ok. We waded out to chest deep water where I could instruct him and hold the ski as he got on. If he was to fall off, releasing the throttle would automatically kill the engine. His parents cheered him on from the shore as he tried again, and again, to get off his knees and stand up on the ski. It would drag him along behind as he circled around, returning to me for more help. He didn't give up. He eventually succeeded and rode the ski away. I waded back to shore feeling pleased at his success.

"He's in heaven out there," his parents said, with a proud grin on their faces. "Thank you for doing this!" That jet ski lesson made my week's trip worthwhile, and I learned that vacationing alone wasn't so bad after all.

I've often wondered if, like my son, the opportunity to experience the excitement of a water sport may have instilled a new passion for this young man. We never know how something we do, or maybe something we say, might affect another person, — in a good way — or a negative way.

As I thought about that notion, I recalled the words from the teen boy at my high school, how his negative comment affected my life for so many years. That one comment created the response to self-consciously cover my mouth, fearing that someone else might criticize my smile.

I also recalled another conversation many years later, in my adult life. This conversation was with an elderly gentleman, as we stood side by side in a grocery checkout line. He'd said something that made me laugh so spontaneously that I didn't have time to cover my mouth. I was shocked at his words.

"Young lady, you have the most beautiful smile!"

I'd once told my dentist about the high school incident. He tried to reassure me I had a slight overbite, not buck teeth. The dentist's attempt to reassure me didn't change my smile habit, but the gentleman's comment in the grocery store changed my life forever.

I will never know if that teen continued to enjoy water sports. Likewise, the gentleman in the grocery store never knew how his kind words impacted my life. He gave me the courage to break my habit. Since then, I often hear comments like, "I love your smile" or "There's that beautiful smile!" I have discovered a beautiful smile has nothing to do with the structure of your teeth; it has everything to do with the genuine personality behind it.

Everything we do — good, bad, or indifferent, sends a wave rolling out of sight, to a place we may never see or feel. But, that one gesture may change someone's life forever.

∞∞∞

Me on a bike ride.

∞ ∞ ∞

Game night at my house - 1997.

∞∞∞

Tik Tok

E ventually I did begin to date but I didn't date anyone from our group, so nobody won that earlier bet.

As our group's average age crept closer to 50, my 50th birthday loomed on the horizon, like a dark cloud. I became fixated on it, worrying that 50 sounded old, especially for dating. My son, Stephen, couldn't grasp my anxiety.

"Why is turning 50 such a big deal?" he asked.

"Who wants to date a 50 year-old woman?"

"A 50 year-old man," he responded matter-of-factly.

"No, they don't! They want to date a 30 year-old woman!"

But 50 arrived, and I survived. I insisted that no party be planned on my behalf. I was glad to still be living at this age but I didn't want to celebrate the occasion, or draw attention to the age. After being single for 11 years, my list of requirements for the perfect man had grown long. I'd become independent and set in my ways. I had not met anyone who came even close to my list — I doubted I ever would. Our group of single friends dwindled as many began to marry — often to someone else within the group. The activities shifted to couples-based events. Feeling like the fifth-wheel, I began to withdraw from that social circle.

Then one day Brian Martin reappeared from the past. His bronze Portuguese-Japanese skin contrasted with his white hair, giving him a handsome look. I met Brian seven years earlier, when he coached René's softball team. Brian was also the father-figure who walked René down the aisle to marry Stephen. I hadn't seen him since their wedding.

Brian had recently purchased property six miles out of Grants Pass, in the Merlin district. He hired my son Stephen to do the excavation work for him. It was softball season and, since Brian had coached René's team some years prior, Stephen invited him to the game.

"You should come to René's game tonight. My mom will be there. You remember her — and she's still single."

Brian did show up. We joked, laughed and visited throughout the game. At one point during the conversation, I'd mentioned growing up in the country; riding bikes and target practicing. That sparked his interest and he invited me to go to the shooting range with him.

"That would be fun. I haven't shot a gun since John and I used to go skeet shooting, many years ago." Several days later, Brian picked me up and we drove to the range.

Brian was a retired Marine. He'd spent 27 years as an instructor; marksmanship, scuba diving, Women's Marine softball team; and other activities. Instructing was ingrained in his nature after all those years. He spent the first hour at the range instructing; safety lessons and showing me how to hold the gun, before we got off a single shot. My first half-dozen shots were close to the bullseye. He seemed surprised with my accuracy.

One day I invited him to come to my house for a swim. I had a 24-foot round, above ground pool, partially surrounded by a cedar deck.

"Do you know all your swim strokes?" Brian questioned me as we climbed into the pool. Immediately, I recalled our first date on the shooting range and the hour of instructions. I knew how to answer this question. I gave him the evil eye and responded,

"No. And at my age I don't intend to learn them." I dismissed the subject before he could proceed to show me. We spent a lot of time together throughout the summer. We played on a co-ed softball team, spent time at the river, and went boating with Stephen and René. Some of the gals on René's softball team loved to tease with, "He's a good catch, Esther, don't let him get away."

In spite of spending time together, I wasn't ready to be considered boyfriend/girlfriend and I made that clear to Brian early on. One evening as he interacted with my sister and nieces on my patio, I enjoyed the laughter and fun we all had together. I began to think, *he does have some good qualities; he'd probably make a good husband; he's good looking; he's active.* By the end of that evening, before he got in his truck to leave, I asked him,

"Are you still interested in upgrading our relationship to boyfriend/girlfriend status?" I laughed as I asked him.

"Yes!"

He proposed that Fall and I accepted. We set a wedding date for the following summer. I downsized my belongings in preparation of combining households. I put my home on the market.

Our July 19, 2003, wedding day was a comedy of errors, and in the long run, maybe an error altogether. We spent hours decorating the reception hall the night before; filling balloons with helium and attaching long streamers that would flutter through the air as we danced among them. When we arrived the next morning, the floor was covered with balloons, streamers still intact. They no longer floated. Stephen offered to buy new balloons and air them up in time for the wedding.

"We still have a tank of helium," he said. After my initial reaction of panic, I made an attitude adjustment.

"Don't worry about it. We'll leave them where they are and dance around them.

The wedding ceremony was held under the awnings of a large patio, at the fairgrounds. Glass doors at the back of the patio provided the entrance to the reception hall.

My bridesmaids were my daughter-in-law, René, and my good friends, Sharon Canfield and Megan Toch. The groomsmen were former military friends of Brian's. Larry and Stephen walked me halfway down the aisle where Chris and Duane were seated. The two older boys dropped behind me as Chris and Duane walked me the rest of the way, ending at the altar with all four. When asked "who gives this bride," the four boys answered, "we do." The vows were recited.

"The couple will now exchange rings," Pastor Don —who was the husband of my good friend and co-worker, Beverly Schuman — held out his hand for the ring. Brian turned to his best man. Tom shook his head, his shoulders shrugged as he raised his hands in question.

"Nobody gave me the rings," he whispered to Brian. I brought the rings to the wedding that morning. Distracted by the deflated balloons, I'd set them down in the reception hall.

"Opps! They're on the table with the guest book!" I laughed as I pointed to the door behind all the guests. Larry ran back, retrieved the rings, and the wedding proceeded. By the conclusion of the ceremony, the guests were dabbing sweat from their foreheads as the July temperatures were reaching for the 100 degree mark.

The reception was lovely, and air conditioned. Guests danced; we had open mic time; and toasts were made. After the guests left and family members helped clean the reception hall, we made a late evening, four-hour drive to Portland where we'd reserved a hotel room. We were scheduled for an early morning flight to Hawaii.

We arrived at our wedding suite — and realized we should not have trusted an advertisement without checking the reviews. There was nothing special about the room — and it was on the low side of average. We were too exhausted to make a fuss after the long drive. We chalked it up to a lesson learned, set the alarm for an early morning flight and crashed.

When we arrived in Oahu, we picked up a rental car. I promptly fell asleep until we arrived at our cozy beach front cabin. Brian carried our luggage in and found me sprawled across the bed, sound asleep. I took Dramamine to keep me from getting motion sick on the five-hour flight. The drug kept me sleeping until 2 pm on that arrival date. Once the medication wore off we enjoyed snorkeling, beach trips, sightseeing and all the tourist attractions Oahu offered. Brian was born and raised in Hawaii, so he knew his way around the island; places to go and places to avoid.

Brian had a Black Belt in TaeKwonDo martial arts. He convinced me, and my son Christopher — who was married and living in Grants Pass at the time — to join the classes. Both Chris and I moved up the rank of belts quickly because we attended back-to-back classes, four to five days a week. Within the first year, we both tested and received our First-Degree Black Belts. I later acquired an instructor's collar, certifying me to assist in teaching classes or filling in for an instructor. Additional classes certified me to teach self-defense. Chris returned to the Portland area where he opened his own martial arts studio, moving through the ranks, and eventually obtaining his Fourth-Degree Black Belt.

I invested money, from the sale of my home, into Brian's property. We added an oversized garage, a carport, recreation room where he could give private martial art lessons, a patio, pergola and hot tub, all to enhance the property, along with landscaping. The home sat on four-acres of forested land.

In the Spring of 2004, we made a six-week, cross-country trip, pulling our 30-foot fifth wheel. We visited as many historic sites as we could along the way: Custer's battleground, Mt Rushmore, Gettysburg, Iwo Jima Memorial, Lincoln Memorial, Washington Memorial, as well as several museums at the Smithsonian. We picked up two of his grandchildren in Shreveport, Louisiana and brought them home with us to spend the rest of the summer.

Brian convinced me to sell my stand-up jet ski that summer. He didn't feel it was safe.

"If Steve buys a boat, then we'll get a sit-on jet ski," he told me. Stephen did buy a boat, and we purchased a three person, 160hp Yamaha Waverunner. Powerful enough to pull a water skier or wakeboarder behind it.

Another thing we enjoyed together was spending time at the R-Ranch in northern California. We were partial owners of the multi-deed dude ranch, 36 miles west of Redding. We could leave our fifth-wheel there for up to 90 days at a time, or we could stay in the small motel for $15 per night. We enjoyed spending our weekends there, riding horses, taking our Grizzly four-wheeler out on trails, target practice, and ending the day with a swim in the pool.

In the Fall of 2004, before Christopher moved back to Portland, he and his wife went with us for a weekend.

"Here, let me help you with that." Chris said as he hopped off of his horse. He assisted Brian with putting his foot back into the stirrup on his saddle. This happened three or four times during the course of our trail ride.

Earlier that morning Brian complained of some weakness in his left ankle and foot as he pulled his boot on. Now he was having difficulty keeping his foot in the stirrup.

When we arrived back at the ranch, we pulled off our riding boots and slipped into our swimsuits and flip flops. As we walked to the pool, Brian's flip flop kept coming off his left foot.

"I can't seem to clench my toes tight enough to hold it on," he complained.

When we got back to Grants Pass, he called his doctor. They ran some tests.

"You've had a minor stroke," they told him. "And your carotid artery is 90% blocked." Brian recalled a time, about a week earlier, when he was standing at the kitchen island, reading the newspaper that was spread out across it.

"I was standing there reading and all of a sudden I fell to the floor," he said. He had no other symptoms and didn't give it any more thought. The doctor suspects that fall was when he had the stroke.

His symptoms appeared minor. His left ankle was weak, creating the slightest bit of limp, noticeable only if you were aware of it. He is left-hand dominant. He discovered he also had difficulty writing with his left hand. Those symptoms were things that life can be adjusted around — or so I thought. Little by little he began to withdraw from activities.

The following summer of 2005, we made a second trip to Hawaii for our second anniversary.

"When I tried to snorkel, I felt like I was going around in circles because I couldn't kick normally," he complained.

When we arrived home from Hawaii, he withdrew from nearly everything. I became concerned. He preferred to stay home rather than go anywhere, even to our traditional Friday night Mexican dinner with Stephen and his family. He helped with martial arts occasionally, but all other activities he withdrew from. He wasn't interested in going to the R-Ranch either. He seemed content to spend the day on the couch, watching television. I assumed he was self conscious — sure that everyone would notice his stroke symptoms since he'd always been an overachiever. He seemed to lose all motivation. The chores around the property were being ignored. I'd find myself coming home from work and trying to take care of the chores in the evenings. Our marriage was on a downhill spiral and I couldn't seem to get him to discuss it. I had learned by now that communication was a must.

"I don't want to argue," he'd say.

"I don't want to either, but we need to do something. And I don't know what to do unless we talk about it." That's as far as I could get. He'd want to put it off until "another day."

It was July 2006 when I came home from work, then went outside in the 100-degree heat to weedeat the overgrown grass on our forested property, afraid it would become a fire hazard. Soaked with sweat and frustrated, I went inside where Briain watched television in the cool, air-conditioned room.

"We need to talk about our marriage," I snapped. I tried to sound calm but I couldn't summon that side of me at that moment.

"Do we have to do it now?"

"Well when *is* a good time?" I didn't want to take no for an answer. He turned the volume down on the television. His cold reply matched the coldness in my voice.

"You always want to talk during the best part of the movie!"

"Forget it."

I went out to the patio glider, sat in the shade of the pergola, and sulked for a while. I thought maybe he'd follow me to talk but he didn't. I probably spent an hour questioning myself: *Do I even love him? Did I ever love him? Or did I convince myself that I loved him?* I recalled those thoughts prior to his proposal: *He's retired. He's fun. He's good looking, energetic, and has some good husband qualities.* Most of my friends were married, I was still single. *Did that influence me?* I wondered, *Maybe the tik tok, tik tok of getting older drowned out any rationale in my decision to get married.* I wasn't sure of the answers. What I did know was that if love existed early on, it had been buried by now. Our relationship didn't resemble anything even similar to when we were dating or first married.

We didn't discuss our marriage until a week later. It was three years and three days after our wedding date when I suggested we go separate ways.

"If that's what you want to do, then let's do it," was his only reply. We spent the next several months selling items, and separating belongings. We split everything 50/50 to be fair with one another. He moved to the east coast to be closer to his kids. I stayed in the house until it sold, then I bought another house in Grants Pass.

I always suspected Brian was depressed over the slight hindrance of his dominant, left hand and foot. I didn't realize until years after we divorced that strokes can also cause a personality change. I believe that was true in Brian's case. The person I dated and married was a completely different person than the man I divorced. Fortunately, we parted on friendly terms, and he occasionally stays in touch.

Sometimes, the hardest thing to learn
is which bridge to burn and which to cross.

∞ ∞ ∞

Me as a Black Belt martial artist. 2004

∞ ∞ ∞

Chapter Fourteen

Just Enough

H ere I was, single again. Sharon moved off to Texas with the love of her life, Jerry Lakatos. I stayed in touch with some of my former single friends, though I seldom got together with them since they'd married. It was the beginning of a new chapter in my life. I decided to place my focus on opening a few more doors, peeking outside to see if the risks were feasible, and taking advantage of available opportunities.

———

As I breezed through the church bulletin, two words jumped off the page — SPEECH CLASS. As I headed out the door, I raised my hand in a gesture to throw the bulletin in the trash. Instead, I paused, tucked it into my purse, and drove home. I tossed it on my dresser in a dismissive manner. Several times over the course of the week, I picked it up and read the blurb. The Toastmasters were offering a four-week introduction to public speaking. A little voice tugged at me to take action. When I attempted to speak in public, I trembled, to the point of my teeth chattering. *I really need this class... and it's free.* With the class being offered on Sunday afternoons, there was no excuse not to take it. I called the number and signed up before I could change my mind again.

Week one: Introduce myself with a little background while standing at the podium. I wanted to do it from my chair, right where I was sitting, but that wasn't the protocol. I could have stated, "My name is Esther, and I'm shy," but I didn't. Everyone who spoke that day was nervous. *Why wouldn't they be?* I thought. *We're all here for the same reason.*

At the end of week four, I joined the Toastmasters club. I attended weekly meetings for the next two years. I served as the Public Relations officer during the second year, posting club updates on their social media page.

The Club taught me to take a deep breath and pause to calm my nerves, which helped me avoid my usual habit of speeding up my speech as I progressed. We were also taught to eliminate filler words like 'and' and 'um,' which often serve as a crutch to fill awkward silences. Our instructors emphasized that pauses are perfectly fine, allowing the audience to absorb what's been said. In fact, a well-timed pause can be more effective than rushing to fill the silence. This resonated with me, especially when I recalled a Sunday sermon by an associate pastor. His nervousness was palpable as he sped through his delivery, leaving me struggling to grasp the message. The Toastmasters' guidance helped me understand why: the pastor hadn't paused enough to let his words sink in.

Toastmasters didn't cure my nervousness but now I know how to control it when I speak to a group. My son, Duane, assured me that being nervous in front of a crowd is natural.

"Even as a pastor and a state representative, I sometimes feel nervous before speaking." Duane told me. I discovered that the nerves like to crawl across my skin before I speak. Once I get started, they calm down. As in all things, practice makes perfect and I'll continue to work at it.

———

It was in 2010 when I woke up in the middle of the night and couldn't get back to sleep. That's not unusual for me. I have bouts of insomnia. I turned over, fluffed my pillow, and tried to go back to sleep. *This is weird!* The thoughts going through my mind all rhymed. *I don't even like poetry!* I grumbled to myself. In exasperation, I reached over to my nightstand and flipped on the light. I put my glasses on, climbed out of bed and gathered a pen and tablet from the desk in a nearby room. I went back to my bed, leaned against my fluffed pillow, and began to write down the thoughts:

> *At midnight, my time is right,*
> *not during the day, I heard him say.*
> *Just when I want to get some sleep,*
> *That's when the Lord is sure to speak.*
> *So Lord, direct me in the night,*
> *because I know your time is right.*

I was no stranger to journaling. At times I'd journal my prayers. When I struggled with things, journaling served as emotional therapy. I've gone through phases of journaling throughout my lifetime. I began using my time of insomnia to journal in rhyme. I joined an online poetry group, and began to post my writing. I entered poems in on-line contests. The awards were stickers being placed on our poems within the group. Basically, a source for bragging rights, although I continued keeping this journey a secret. I felt embarrassed to admit I wrote poetry. *Who really likes poetry — or writes it?* When I did mention it to someone, I said, "I write in rhyme," avoiding the word "poetry." I received many stickers while the writing phase lasted, the course of about eight months. After the phase ended, I eventually deleted the mass amount of poems I'd written. I kept only a handful — ones with a theme that centered around healing, and keeping my faith through times of struggles. I created a small pamphlet with them, giving them out on occasion to friends who are struggling. The title: *Keeping the Faith, in the midst of the trials.*

———

"Why do you do that, Esther?" Carol's voice was sharp as she reprimanded me. She paused only a second before continuing, "Why can't you just say, 'Thank You' and leave it at that? You could just let me believe you're wearing a beautiful, expensive ring."

I didn't know how to accept a compliment gracefully. Compliments made me feel awkward — they directed attention to something specific about me. My response would often be negative. While having lunch with Carol and another friend, she picked up my hand, admiring my ring.

"What a gorgeous ring," she said.

"Oh, it's just cheap zirconia," I answered. I flushed at the attention directed at me. She dropped my hand, glared at me, and gave me a much needed reprimand.

"I don't know why I do that. It makes me feel awkward when someone gives me a compliment. I guess I don't know what I'm supposed to say." I told her, knowing I deserved her sharp tongue.

"Well, next time just say, 'thank you.' You don't have to say more. When you say, 'it's just a cheap ring' it makes me feel awkward. How am I supposed to respond to that comment?"

"You're right. I've never thought of it that way. I'll work on it," I told her. And I did. I'm grateful for her boldness in speaking up. A short, polite "thank you" has simplified my life.

———

I could envision it so clearly in my mind. My long hair flowed in the cool gentle breeze. My toned legs formed long strides as my arms pumped gently to the cadence. I moved along the roadside as gracefully as a gazelle.

I admired runners. Deciding I could be a runner if I set my mind to it, I signed up for a 5k. The poster gave a date eight weeks away. I'd heard of the C25K (couch to 5k) app – a training program that prepares you to run a 5k in nine weeks. I downloaded the app to my phone. If I trained four days a week, rather than the suggested three, I'd be ready to run the 5k by week eight. There was no room for slacking. I was anxious to get started.

Day one: I barely made it through the first 60-second run and was relieved when the 90-second walk started. It ended way too soon... back to running. Grumbling to myself for making this decision, I nearly gave it up... until I realized I only had one more set to complete. *I can do this!* When I finished, a feeling of triumph surged through my body. My accomplishment energized me to hit the road on day two – which wasn't much easier. *This running stuff isn't what I visualized in my mind!*

Thump, thump, thump, my feet hit the pavement as I wiped the sweat dripping from my brow. There was no gentle breeze blowing my hair. *Thump, thump, thump*, I continued down the road. My legs cramped as they screamed stop! *Thump, thump...* *Opps*, I nearly sprained an ankle stepping off the edge of the pavement... *thump, thump, thump...* like the sound — and speed — of an elephant, I slowly made my way through the day's training program.

Why would anyone want to do this to their body? The thought crossed my mind every day as I trained. *But they do, and I can do it too.* I discovered why they did it. It's the euphoria of completion at the end. A feeling of accomplishment. But in the midst of the journey, I wasn't feeling any of those things.

There were days when my daughter-in-law, René, jogged alongside me. When she was tired of jogging, she'd change to a fast-paced walk. Even then, she was able to keep pace with me. My slow jog didn't follow a straight line. I meandered like a drunken sailor. No matter how much my body ached, no matter how much I wanted to quit, my desire to finish and feel that euphoria of completion, kept me going.

"You can walk too, Esther. You don't have to run the entire distance in a 5k." I kept hearing that statement. My goal was to run, or at least jog, the entire length. If I walked any portion of it, then this gruesome training would be senseless. I completed the training in eight weeks. I didn't miss a day. It did get easier as the weeks went by but the gazelle never showed up. The nagging urge to quit in the midst of each run remained. Regardless, the important thing to me was not to give up – and I didn't. When race day arrived, I jogged the entire distance – like a drunken sailor – crossing the finish line 40 minutes later. I didn't care about the length of time it took. My ultimate goal was to keep my pace, not walk, and cross the finish line. My reward: Knowing I stuck with it; I didn't give up; and I completed what I'd set out to do. An extra bonus was at the end of the eight weeks, I was fit and trim, and in the best physical condition of my life. That was the extent of my running career. I participated in other 5k fun runs with friends but we would walk and run, as we socialized and supported the event. In my repertoire of things I've done, I can now say..."I ran a 5k."

———

"Are you ready?" I hear the faint yell. I nod my head yes. The boat takes off, gaining speed. The rope rips the handle out of my hands, plunging me face first into the water. I cough and spit out murky lake water as I struggle to flip the wakeboard over — which is still attached to my feet — trying to put myself in a face-up position. The boat circles around and I grab the rope for a second try. I nod my head, the boat engine roars, the rope pulls tight lifting me up. I skim across the lake on the wakeboard. The water sprays my face, the wind whips my hair. I shake my head trying to remove the wet hair from my mouth. I don't trust letting go with either hand, even long enough to push the hair aside. I bounce and wobble until I can cross the wake into smoother water. That's where I stay. Most attempts to cross back and forth meant the end of the ride for me. If the water is calm, I can ride the distance of the reservoir. If it's choppy, the ride is shortened. Will I ever be able to ride like Stephen, who jumps the wake, spins around, and can even carry a young beginner on the wakeboard with him? Never! And that's ok with me. My goal is to be able to say, "I can still get up!"

What if I fall? — Oh, but darling, what if you fly?
If you never try, you'll never know.

———

I never had the drive to master, or become an expert, at any activity I've attempted. Once I accomplished the know-how and could do the activity enough to enjoy it, I didn't take it to the next level. I've always been a little embarrassed of my lack of perseverance, considering myself an underachiever.

Kurt Vonnegut is an American writer of novels, short stories, plays and non-fiction. When I read an article written about him, it changed my opinion of myself and my many activities.

Kurt was age 15 when he was prompted by a fellow co-worker to talk about his many cultural activities in which he participated.

214

"Wow, that's amazing!" the co-worker said as he listened to Kurt's accomplishments.

"Oh no, but I'm not any good at ANY of them." Kurt responded.

Kurt said the co-worker's response blew his mind because no one had ever said anything like it to him before:

"I don't think being good at things is the point of doing them. I think you've got all these wonderful experiences with different skills, and that all teaches you things and makes you an interesting person, no matter how well you do them."

"That conversation changed my life," Kurt said.

I could totally relate to Kurt's story. I'd been pleased I could do many things enough to enjoy them, but the enjoyment was always tainted by the underachiever title that lurked in the back of my mind for many years. After reading Kurt's story, that label disappeared, and I'm pleased to be able to say:

*"I can do a lot of things enough to enjoy them, but
I'm far from an expert on any of them!"*

———

Me wakeboarding.

∞ ∞ ∞

Even the Small Stuff

I shifted my weight from one hip to the other. My legs cramped, longing to be stretched. I didn't want to inconvenience the two people beside me by climbing over their laps to stretch my legs or use the restroom. Instead, I shifted, I stretched – as best I could. I tried not to crowd the shoulder-to-shoulder elbow space. I cupped my tablet in my hands, resting it on my lap to read. *Why did I choose the window seat?* I always chose a window seat on the plane. I liked the aerial view. Now I regret my choice. It would be a 10-hour flight to Amsterdam. *At some point I'll have to climb over them and make my way to the restroom. When I do, I'll stand for a spell.* After a short delay in Amsterdam, we'd have another 10-hour flight to Kampala, Uganda, another window seat to dread.

A mission trip had always interested me, but I never dreamed I'd actually go. When I received a call from my son, Duane, who was the mission pastor at River Valley Community Church, in Grants Pass, Oregon, I didn't hesitate to join his team. I immediately scheduled vacation time from work. The trip was four months out, time to get all the necessary travel shots, a passport, and cultural training.

I was prone to motion sickness. I wore a patch, but I felt nervous now since I was inconveniently stuck in my seat. I checked the slot on the seat in front of me — thankful there was a vomit bag in case an emergency need arose. I didn't think landing in Kampala would come soon enough. When we did, I was extra grateful the bag was still in the slot, unused.

Kampala is the capital of Uganda, located in the southern part of the country. Our team's destination was Koboko, located in the north, near the Sudan border. We were a team of 20. We gathered our luggage from the airport and boarded a dilapidated bus. The suitcases were crammed snuggly in the undercarriage. We made our way to available straight-backed, hard seats among a nearly-full busload of people. This was another shoulder-to-shoulder ride for seven long hours in 90-degree weather — and no air-conditioning. We faced a daunting dilemma: keep the windows closed and swelter in the oppressive heat, — which felt like being trapped in an oven set to a scorching temperature — or roll down the windows and endure the choking red dust that billowed in like smoke from a chimney. Neither option offered much comfort. I opted for the window up but others rode with a partially open window. It was a combination of sweltering and coughing.

Rest stops were welcome for a breath of fresh air and squatty potty breaks – a hole dug in the ground, a brick placed on each side to plant your feet, to do your business.

At each stop we were met by a swarm of vendors who sold chicken-on-a-stick and various other street foods. Many reached their arms through open windows hoping to sell to those who didn't leave the bus. I didn't purchase anything on the trip north but on our return trip a week later, I did try the chicken-on-a-stick, and it was delicious. The long, hot journey ended in Koboko and our luggage was pulled from the undercarriage storage space. Without name tags it would have been hard to distinguish one person's luggage from another's. Each item was identically clothed in a thick layer of red dirt.

Koboko, as with much of Africa, didn't have running water. The showers in our motel were gravity-fed, coming from water tanks placed on the roof. The sun heated the water. The four-post double bed I shared with my roommate Joy was canopied with mosquito nets, hopeful protection from malaria.

Calloused bare feet were the number one form of transportation in Koboko. Mamas walked down the street barefoot with their babies and toddlers tucked into colorful fabric slings, wrapped around their backs. Bicycles or motor scooters, carried two, three, or four riders. Roads were littered with paper and garbage. One disposal technique was to place the trash in a pile and burn it.

Our typical meal consisted of freshly butchered chicken, served with beans and a small piece of homemade pita-style bread. One evening we had a second option: goat-meat stew.

"I'll try a little." I told the young girl who politely gave me the choice. It was my first time eating anything made with goat meat. It had a dense texture, and a slight gamey taste. I liked the experience of something new, but I decided: if given the option again, I'll choose chicken.

Ugandans are hard-working people. Michael proved that to me. He had a bright shiny smile and chocolate brown skin. He was one of the staff members at the orphanage. As our week in Koboko neared its end, he graciously offered to wash our dirty, dusty, sweat-soaked clothes. We all chipped in money for the service. I watched him balance and tote the huge laundry bag away on his bicycle. When he returned the next day, every piece was clean and neatly folded.

"Is the laundromat close by?" I asked Tom Criswell, our team leader.

"Esther, there's no running water in Koboko," he reminded me. I threw my hands in the air, in disbelief. I had forgotten that fact. Michael washed clothes for 20 people by hand, line-dried, folded and returned them.

Our safety was a concern for Edson, the local Chief of Police. He insisted on escorting us every time we left our motel. A team of 20 missionaries, plus Edson, squeezed into a van marked Capacity 12. We sat on seats, laps and the floor on our way to the orphanage. There we spent time with the children, singing, dancing, playing games, and handing out the clothes we brought — something for everyone.

We had a retired dentist who volunteered his expertise in Uganda. He was unable to perform fillings or other dental work but he was able to extract teeth that couldn't be saved, for members of the Koboko community. Our team doctor held classes at the primary and secondary schools educating students about AIDS, a great health concern in Africa. Each of our team members took two suitcases. One with our personal clothes (long skirts or pants for the girls, no shorts), the other carried children's clothes and shoes for orphans, mosquito nets for health clinics, and reading glasses.

We held an eyeglass clinic which was open to the entire community. A long line of pencil thin bodies patiently stood for hours, hoping to receive a pair of glasses to improve their vision. We used eye exam charts to test their vision and provided simple readers appropriate to their tested level.

I stood nose-to-nose with weather-beaten faces as I fitted them with glasses. I watched eyes glisten with tears, saw toothless grins spread across faces, received hugs of gratitude, ecstatic at the detail they could now see. I continually dabbed at my own damp eyes. One elderly woman ran the back of her hand across her dusty, now mud-streaked, cheeks. She spoke in broken English. She shared that she hadn't been able to read anything in over a year. Now she would be able to read to her grandchildren again. Over 200 Ugandan residents received reading glasses on that trip.

Our team delivered mosquito nets to the ill-equipped medical clinics in the northern area of Uganda and a pickup full of 50-pound bags of flour, beans, and other staples to a single woman who, independently, took children into her home and cared for them. Their ages ranged from infants to young teens.

Most of our team returned to the states after that first week in Koboko. Duane, I, and six other team members stayed another week in Jenga, near the southern border of Uganda where we had time to explore the area between visits with college students and the Amani Baby Cottage, an orphan home for children under six.

I studied the weathered hull of the traditional wooden canoe-style boat as I eagerly awaited my turn to climb aboard. *This boat has seen a lot of trips up this river!* I thought. I settled onto the rough-hewn bench, partially shaded by a frayed blue tarpaulin nailed to sturdy wooden posts. A sense of excitement and anticipation washed over me. *I'm actually going to be riding on the Nile River!*

A small outboard motor, operated by our Ugandan guide, propelled us slowly against the current as we made our way up the river. I watched the slow, graceful, movement of the great white egrets' wide wingspans as they moved along the river's shore in search of a meal. A monitor lizard, roughly six feet in length, swam in front of us as he crossed the river. Lush green shrubs lined much of the moist, fertile river bank. The Nile River flows over 6,800 kilometers — 4,000 miles — bending and stretching through the heart of Africa before it reaches the Mediterranean Sea. When our guided tour ended, Duane and I had our picture taken in front of a sign that read: The Source of the Nile — Jenga — World's Longest River.

After spending a morning at the Amani Baby Cottage, we browsed the shops in downtown Jenga. Tom Criswell, our team leader, visited with a college-age man on the street corner. Tom invited him to join us for lunch. We went to a tiny cafe close by. There was seating for about 10 inside and there were several small tables outside the door. We placed our order: hamburgers, fries, and warm bottled sodas. We didn't drink the local water, or use ice cubes made from that water. Bottled sodas were not kept refrigerated. Tom treated our guest to lunch, who appeared to thoroughly enjoy his meal. When he finished eating, he told us that hamburger was the first he had ever eaten and it was also his first experience of eating in a cafe.

My trip to Africa was an experience of a lifetime for me. It opened my eyes to the things I've taken for granted in the United States, such as trash removal and clean, running water. Every day I look around me and feel gratitude for the blessings in my life... all the things I overlooked prior to visiting a third-world country. I learned to appreciate even the small stuff.

Twice, I had the pleasure of hosting three young girls for the weekend in my home. They were a part of the African Children's Choir visiting Grants Pass. The first time was before my trip to Africa and the other, after. All were under age 12.

"Can we take a bath instead of a shower?" the oldest girl shyly asked in her reasonably fluent English. I adjusted the water temperature for them and went out of the room as the three began to eagerly undress, anxious for the opportunity. I heard the water run for a short time, then shut off. I knocked on the door to check on them. "Come in!" I heard through giggles. I opened the door and saw three little girls, their wide eyes sparkling as they looked at me; their smiles nearly too broad to fit their little faces. Their giggles would warm the coldest of hearts. Then I noticed — they were having that much fun in one inch of water.

"Oh, honey, fill it up!" I turned the water back on and filled the tub. They spent an hour playing, and enjoying, a luxury they didn't have at home. Water is not wasted in Africa. After drinking a cup of tea, one of the girls washed her cup under a trickling faucet while quickly cleaning her hands at the same time.

Gratitude unlocks the fullness of life.
It turns what we have into enough, and more;
it turns denial into acceptance; chaos to order;
confusion to clarity. It can turn a meal into a feast; a
house into a home; a stranger into a friend.

Melody Beattie

∞∞∞

Eyeglass clinic in Koboko, Uganda, Africa 2012

Me at Amani Baby Cottage - 2012

∞ ∞ ∞

Me and Duane at the, Source of the Nile River,
Uganda, Africa - February 2012.

∞ ∞ ∞

San Juan Islands

I often made day trips alone with my Waverunner. I'd launch the jet ski, find a spot on the beach for my blanket, then allow the cool spray of water to dampen my body as I rode across the lake. Feeling cool and refreshed, I'd return to my blanket where I'd sprawl out, letting the sun toast my skin, hoping for a golden brown. My music played at a low, nearly hypnotic level, allowing me to drift into a light sleep. The sizzle of heat on my skin signaled me to get back on the Waverunner and cool off before the golden brown turned to lobster red. A few laps around the lake left me ready to repeat the cycle.

Those daily trips were easy to do alone. The trip to Redding broke the ice for solo vacations. In Redding, I stayed in a motel. This time, I prepared myself to camp solo. I read an article about the San Juan Islands. An island vacation appealed to me. I didn't mention it to anyone, not yet convinced I wouldn't talk myself out of it. Camping alone would be a big step and the San Juan Islands seemed a little farther out of my comfort zone than the three hours to Redding. By the first of July, keeping images of what it could be like in my mind, I felt more secure about the decision. I mentioned it to my long-time friend Megan Toch. She and I became close friends when she worked at the law firm, where I worked. After she went to work at her husband's plumbing business, we continued our standing Tuesday lunch date for a number of years, and we also spent a cold, foggy weekend together at the Oregon coast.

"Edgewater Christian Fellowship has a group going to the San Juan Islands that same week!" Megan said. "You should go with them." Edgewater had been my church for several years after the boys left home.

I called the church. Yes, they would be going at the end of July and welcomed me to join them. It was unstructured, meaning they would pitch their tents in the group section, eat, and fellowship around the evening campfire together but everyone was on their own for activities. A perfect arrangement for me. I paid $125 for my share of the campsite and meals. What a deal! I set up my tent in a secluded area.

I brought my bicycle and my kayak and scheduled my first-ever zipline adventure. It included eight exhilarating rides over the ziplines with small challenges between each. I took a ferry to Orcas Island. I was told it would be the best area for a good kayaking experience. One of the church members decided to go with me, renting a kayak at the mouth of the bay where we paddled. As the tide went out, an array of colorful brown, yellow and purple starfish speckled the banks, clinging to the rocks until the tide waters returned. My bicycle stayed in camp. The hilly roads on the island were steeper than I wanted to peddle.

The Redding vacation and the San Juan Islands set the course for future vacations: long weekend camp trips that included tent camping alone at Dorena Lake where I paddled the slow flowing Row River and bicycled the 34-mile Rails-to-Trails bike path into Cottage Grove. That trip included a number of covered bridges along the way. On another tent camping trip at Silver Falls State Park, I hiked the Trails of Ten Falls, visiting all 10 waterfalls along the pathway.

It really is ok to spend some quality time alone. By now, I realized that fact.

Fill your life with adventures before things.

∞ ∞ ∞

Me (fourth from left) - zipline on San Juan Island.

Me and Megan at the Oregon coast.

∞ ∞ ∞

Chapter Fifteen

Embrace the Age

"You're an amazing woman, Mom. Why don't you embrace the age and enjoy it?" Larry confronted me as I whined about getting older. The years passed in a whirlwind of activities, changes and growth since I turned 50. Now I faced 60, which seemed to be approaching faster than I wanted.

My birthday is October 6th. In September, I'd spent Labor Day weekend with Larry's family, a Black Belt Training Camp weekend with Christopher, and a weekend of boating with Stephen's family.

"Mom," Duane said, "you've spent time with all the other boys recently. We get you for your birthday weekend."

He wouldn't tell me the plan. He secretly arranged with my boss for me to have Friday off. As the date got closer, he told me about the arrangement. He knew there may be things I needed to take care of before having an unexpected day off work. Friday morning Duane, Dusti, their two toddlers, and I, put our bags in the car and headed out for the weekend. As we took routes that headed toward the Oregon coast, I assumed we would be camping at the coast. When I asked if that was the destination, I received no confirmation.

"No, we're not camping at the coast," he said. "Don't ask. You'll

228

see when we get there."

As we neared the town of Yachats, I was surprised when he turned onto a long, paved driveway that led up the hillside. We parked in front of a huge two-story house with a three-car garage. I suspected someone loaned this extravagant home to Duane for the weekend since he was a pastor at our church, but he still wouldn't confirm my suspicions. Duane put the key in the lock and pushed the door open.

"Surprise!" Larry and his family stood inside the entrance with big smiles. After a round of warm hugs, kisses, and happy birthday wishes, they gave me a tour of the stunning luxury home. The main floor boasted a gourmet kitchen and a spacious open floor plan that combined the dining room and living room. Large picture windows framed a breathtaking, full view of the ocean. The house had seven bedrooms spread across two floors, including one downstairs room with five cozy bunk beds. The recreation room in the basement was a fun zone, equipped with pinball machines and games. As I stood at the window, taking in the incredible view, I noticed a small silver car making its way up the driveway.

"Is that Christopher?" I asked, unable to control the excitement in my voice. I recognized his car. Everyone grinned in acknowledgement.

"Is Stephen coming too?"

"I just talked with him. He's about ten minutes out." Larry answered.

There were 19 of us who shared an incredible weekend together, filled with laughter, connection, and adventure. One of the highlights was a puzzle that we all worked on, taking turns at a child-size table in the dining room. We even sat in kid-sized chairs, adding to the playful atmosphere of working the puzzle! When we weren't looking for a place to insert a puzzle piece, we enjoyed pinball games, hiked trails to the beach, explored tidepools, and shared warm group hugs. The coastal weather was misty, with low clouds on this October weekend, but the weather didn't stop us. One of the most special moments was when my entire family, all 19 of us, for the first time ever, gathered around the same dinner table. And two of my grandchildren met each other for the very first time. When I asked how they could keep this secret, Larry said,

"It wasn't easy. I'm surprised one of us didn't give it away at some point. We've been planning it for months."

During that weekend, Larry's advice about accepting the age and enjoying it made perfect sense. The hardest birthday for me, turning 60, was the best birthday of my life. I took my son's advice after that. Age is a number. Life is amazing. When I turned 70, I reminded myself how fortunate I am to be this age – many people didn't make it this far. I don't celebrate birthdays per se but I don't negate their importance either. Now, I embrace the age and enjoy it.

A wise person knows there are lessons
to be learned from everyone.

∞ ∞ ∞

Meeting Robbie

"**W**ould you like to go jet skiing at Galesville with me today?" I asked my friend, Pia, on a hot Sunday morning.

"I'd love to!" Her only reluctance was that she had plans to visit a friend that afternoon. "Would it be ok to invite her?"

"The more, the merrier!" I replied. That day I spent time with half a dozen new faces. Robbie Cooke was among the friends Pia invited. Like my friendship with Sharon, Robbie and I connected, and soon became inseparable. We cultivated a new circle of single friends, which continued to grow over time. She and I took turns hosting game nights; we explored the outdoors through hikes; we floated the river; we trekked through the hills on snowshoes; and organized whitewater raft trips. We always had a plan for some event on our calendars.

"Let's put it out there," we'd say. "If others join us, great. If not, the two of us will do it together anyway." At times it was just the two of us. Other times we'd have large groups joining. One of our first adventures together was with six other gals when we did a guided snowshoe tour at Crater Lake. It was only my second time on snowshoes. After my first snowshoe trip, which was with Larry and his family on a New Year's Eve, I was hooked.

When summer came we scheduled a whitewater raft trip with several other ladies. The whitewater rafting became an annual co-ed event — each year the group was larger than the previous year.

I like to give Robbie a bad time about her text messages. She talks into her phone, then doesn't put her glasses on to re-read what she said.

"You keep me entertained trying to figure out what your text message is supposed to say." I've told her many times. The one I've never let her live down is when we were at the Oregon coast. She and I were crabbing off the dock. The day before I arrived, she had been crabbing on a boat with friends. While she and I were on the dock, she decided to text her friends and tell them what we were doing. She spoke into her phone and as she was about to hit send, I asked,

"Did you read what you're sending? You know how your text messages turn out sometimes." She looked at her phone to double check her message. It read:

"Esther and I are crapping on the dog today."

Me and Robbie crabbing on the dock.

Robbie has been my close friend and confidant since 2012. We often laugh when we admit — "We never run out of words when we're together!"

I stayed in touch occasionally with some of the gals from my previous group of friends. One such friend was Cheri, and her daughter, Ashley.

Cheri had married and moved to northern California. Her daughter, Ashley, still lived in southern Oregon. While talking on the phone with Cheri one day, she mentioned that Ashley was feeling lonely. I decided to reach out to Ashley and invited her to join me for a movie at Tinseltown theater. As we left the theater, the downpour of rain made the dark night even darker. I struggled to see the dividing lines in a newly revamped intersection. Flashing lights, followed by a brief blast from a siren drew my attention to my rearview mirror. I pulled over. A female officer approached the window.

"Do you know why I pulled you over?" she asked. I didn't know. She explained that I'd made a lane change without signaling and cut someone off.

"I'm sorry. I didn't realize that. I couldn't see any lines because of the rain."

"How much have you had to drink?" She studied my face. I turned to look at Ashley. We both burst into laughter, unable to control ourselves.

"I'm sorry," I apologized to the officer for laughing. "I drank about 32 ounces of cola, with my bag of popcorn. We just came from the movies."

"The reason I asked is because your eyes are red and

bloodshot." She studied my face a little closer.

"It was a chick-flick. We were crying." At this point the officer joined in our laughter.

"Ok. Have a good evening and be careful," she said. She returned to her patrol car and drove away. Ashley and I laughed awhile longer.

I've shared many joyful experiences with friends over the years. Far too many stories to share in this book. I will tell you though, I can relate to the quote of Winnie the Pooh when he said to Piglet:

> *We didn't know we were making memories.*
> *We just thought we were having fun.*

Me and Robbie - 2013

∞ ∞ ∞

∞ ∞ ∞

Contentment

Somewhere I read that a person has as much of a desire to love someone, as the desire to be loved. I tend to believe that is true. People seem to be in love with the idea of being in love.

I spent 19 years as a single woman after John's death. I was single for 11 years before I married Brian, then I was single another eight years at the time an interesting conversation arose between Robbie and I.

"I love my life," I told her, "But it really would be nice if I had someone to share it with." I liked my job and my boss; I was financially comfortable; I enjoyed time with my friends; and I have a wonderful family. I felt secure in the woman I'd become — very independent. I wasn't feeling desperate, or pressured by a ticking clock this time. I simply thought, it would be nice to have someone special in my life.

I had dated a few guys. One relationship — before I married Brian — lasted a year. With his out-of-town work situation and the differences in our personalities, we eventually grew apart. After my divorce from Brian, I dated a guy who lived in Spokane. Long-distance relationships are tough. When we parted ways, I decided a long-distance relationship would never be considered again.

With my niece's wedding planned for September 20, 2014, I planned a week's vacation to attend the ceremony and then visit my son in Seattle. On a whim, I decided to browse Plenty of Fish, an online dating site, and explore profiles in the greater

Seattle area. *I won't contact anyone. I'm just curious if there are any interesting profiles in that area, since I haven't met anyone locally.*

I breezed through tons of photos, none of which warranted opening the profile to read more. I chuckled to myself. *It's a good thing anyway since I don't want a long-distance relationship.* As I was about to give up the Seattle pursuit, one photograph caught my attention. *Hmmmm, I'll open this one.* I was impressed when I read his list of interests: kayaking-*check*, photography-*check*, hiking-*check*, he played guitar-*check-check*, he enjoyed singing and theater-*check. Dang!* The only problem being a 400-mile distance between us. My roots were grounded in Grants Pass, Oregon. My idea of — *I'll check it out but I won't contact anyone* — went out the window. I typed:

"Nice profile. Too bad you live so far away. We have some similar interests. Would have been fun to go for a paddle with you or watch a Seahawks (but preferably Mariners) game together. LOL."

I pondered whether to hit send or delete, wishing he lived closer. I leaned toward delete. *Why send it? ...but what will it hurt if I do?* I wavered between the dos and the don'ts. Giving way to the do, I stabbed the send key before I could change my mind. A swarm of butterflies took flight in my stomach. I stared at the screen, *What have I done?* I had instant regret. I slowly closed the laptop. Leaving it open would create unnecessary stress. I didn't want my attention to be constantly pulled to the screen wondering — *Is there a response?*

Part of me eagerly watched the clock, wanting to give time for a response but anxiously wanting to check -- the other part of me weighed heavily with dread. I put myself in a vulnerable situation, setting myself up to possible rejection — either by no response at all, or lack of interest due to distance — or just plain lack of interest, period. I would understand the long-distance issue. I didn't want a long-distance relationship either, but... facing any rejection would be hurtful. I wondered why I foolishly sent the message.

I took a deep breath, then let it out with a loud sigh as I summoned the courage to open the computer. My heart did a quick *thump!* I had a message. *At least there's a response, but what will it say?* I took another deep breath as I double-clicked the mouse. The screen lit up, revealing the message that would change everything...

"I think you got that backwards. It's too bad YOU live so far away."

To be content doesn't mean you don't desire more,
it means you're thankful for what you have
and patient for what's to come.

Whitewater rafting on the
Deschutes River with friends.

∞∞∞

Part 3 - The Payoff

Chapter Sixteen

Only a Friend

"**F**rom your profile pictures, it looks like you get up this way occasionally to see your family," he went on to say.

"I do. I'm heading that way in two weeks for my niece's wedding, then a visit with my son in Seattle for a few days."

"Why don't we get together for coffee when you're in the area?"

By now I'd learned the importance of communication and, somewhat, learned to speak my mind. If it wasn't a face-to-face conversation, that made it even easier.

"I'd like that. But, to be honest, I'm not interested in a long-distance relationship. Been there, done that." I typed back. I explained about the search being out of curiosity since I'd be making a trip north, and I hadn't met anyone of interest locally.

"I agree, but I'm always in the market for new friends. Why don't you stop by on your way back from Seattle? I can show you around the island."

I exchanged phone numbers with Sean Griffin. That was something I never did with other guys in such short order. But if I was going to meet him in two weeks, I wanted to get to know him over the phone before taking a trip to the island. After a phone call or two, we FaceTimed. He was as charming on FaceTime as his voice sounded over the phone.

Visiting an island intrigued me. The idea of meeting this guy intrigued me. *Shoot, why does he have to live so far away?*

Anderson Island is located at the south end of Puget Sound, accessible only by a 20-minute ferry ride, or private boat. We set a date for the island visit on my return trip from Seattle, much to the concern of my best friend, Robbie.

"Be sure to send me a picture of his license plate!" She insisted.

"I'll give you a call after I get there." I gave Robbie a copy of Sean's photographs, his phone number, and address.

Dark clouds hung low in the sky, threatening a downpour of rain. The ferry rocked as it crashed against the choppy waves, pushing its way toward Anderson Island. My face stung as my hair whipped against it. I could taste the damp, salty air as I stood on the ferry deck. A chill ran through me. I zipped my jacket to my chin and headed back to the car. Using my fingers, I untangled my wind-blown hair.

Sean was in the middle of a photography class with a 10 year-old student when I arrived. He welcomed me with a pleasant introduction and suggested I make myself comfortable while he finished up his class. "...then I'll show you around the island," he said. I was a little too nervous to sit while waiting. Instead, I admired the beauty of the waterfront from his deck. The shrill whistle sound I heard turned out to be that of an eagle; its large wing span gliding toward Eagle Island. The wings flapped gracefully a few times as it settled on the nest in the tallest tree on Eagle Island. I watched seals playfully splashing in the water. This was a view of a magical paradise.

After finishing his class, Sean gave me a tour of the large two-story, five-bedroom house. He had turned the downstairs bedroom into a photography studio. Not only did he shoot sunsets, sunrises, flora, fauna, and wildlife, he also did portraits for upcoming fashion models.

With the household tour complete, we set out to see the island. I learned that Eagle Island was named for Harry Eagle, a member of the Wilkes Expedition in 1841, not because eagles nested there. Island roads were canopied by towering trees. Fir cones and needles covered the road after a recent bout of strong winds. He showed me the major sites along with their history in a nutshell: Population 1,000 year-round with summer vacationers raising the total to approximately 4,000; a small general store carries most items you need on a daily basis; the cafe serves breakfast and lunch, open on Monday evenings for Burger Night; dinner guests can view activity on Lake Josephine while eating at The Lakeshore Restaurant, open evenings only. There are two freshwater lakes on Anderson Island. Lake Josephine, allows non-motorized watercrafts. Lake Florence allows motorized boats and has a popular swimming hole. Numerous small parks line the shores of both lakes.

Historic Johnson Farm continues to care for a small apple orchard, sponsoring an annual Apple Squeeze in the Fall. Two large chicken coops, now remodeled, house a gift shop and vintage items related to the farm's history. The farm also has a large community garden and had plans for an archival building. The latter showcasing Anderson Island's history, and a venue for concerts, art shows, and film festivals.

We finished the driving tour and Sean proposed a hike to Jacob's Point. Since I'd arrived on the island, the clouds had gotten increasingly darker. I worried they might unleash a downpour in the middle of our hike. Normally, I wouldn't mind hiking in the rain, but I was more concerned about making a good first impression. I didn't want to arrive back at his house looking like a drowned rat, especially since we didn't have an umbrella with us. I crossed my fingers the clouds would hold off long enough for us to enjoy the hike without getting soaked. The path zigzagged through shrubs and trees, leading past several viewpoints and eventually to a rocky beach.

"On a clear day you can see the mountain from here." Sean pointed to the hazy horizon. He was referring to Mount Rainier. I soon discovered the common phrase on an uncloudy day: "The Mountain's out today." It doesn't take more than a hazy sky for her to go back into hiding. As we took in the beauty, tiny raindrops splat against my nose and cheeks.

"We should head back," Sean suggested. By the time we reached the car, my hair was wet and flat, and our clothes were damp from the drizzle. Back at the house, as I warmed up by the cozy pellet stove, I spotted Sean's guitar in the dining room. I didn't mention it then, but my mind wandered to my own guitar, stored away in a bedroom closet for years, a reminder of my unfulfilled goal to learn how to play. I attempted to take a class at the college once, but when I discovered I needed to learn music theory and read sheet music, I lost motivation and dropped out. Another time, I hired a friend of Duane's to teach me chords, but my lack of dedication and practice meant I never made progress. The guitar remained a dream to be realized in its case in the closet. *Someday when I retire, I'll learn,* I told myself.

"You can sleep in my room and I'll take the back bedroom," Sean offered. "I want you to have the experience of waking up to that view." He smiled as he motioned to the glass slider door, opening to an upstairs deck overlooking the same Eagle Island view as the downstairs deck. The king-size sleigh bed, placed strategically in the middle of the room, lay directly under the skylight — a viewing source of the stars. I sent a confirmation text to Robbie that all was ok. "I'll be sleeping in his room tonight... while he sleeps in the back bedroom. LOL"

I awoke to the soft glow of dawn through the large glass windows, and the distant sound of a tug boat. I raised myself on my elbows and took in the morning's view that Sean wanted me to see — worthy of opening my eyes at this ungodly morning hour. But, if I wanted to take a walk on the beach before leaving, I needed to get up.

Danielle tug boat pulling a log raft.

There was no sandy beach, but stones covered with barnacle, clam shells, and pieces of small driftwood. When I kicked over a larger stone with the toe of my shoe, tiny hermit crabs scrambled about, trying to relocate to another protective hiding place. As we stood on the beach, Sean surprised me.

"Is it ok if I kiss you?" he nervously asked. Totally out of the scheme of our original plan, I agreed. He placed his lips against mine with a soft, gentle, touch. After a short embrace, we walked to the base of the stairs holding hands. The 46 steep steps were exhausting. I slunk into the comfortable futon on Sean's deck. We had a little time to spare before I needed to get in line to catch the ferry. I wanted to enjoy the water view as long as possible.

"Can I ask you to do something for me, before I leave?"

"Sure." Sean's voice sounded a little hesitant, wondering what the "something" would be.

"Will you play a song for me on your guitar?"

He grinned, went inside, and returned with the guitar and a song book. — At a later date, I realized Sean never turns down an opportunity to sing. I love that about him. — He strummed a few tunes, flipped the pages and began singing the words of an old Everly Brothers' song.

I bless the day I found you
I want to stay around you
Now and forever, let it be me.

I learned that Sean retired from Boeing as a senior manager of Communications; he'd worked 21 years as a journalist, spending 10 years covering the White House, Congress, and the Supreme Court for The Phoenix Gazette, which was later acquired by the Arizona Republic; and twice he was nominated for a Pulitzer Prize. He divorced two years prior to my meeting him. After retiring, he looked for a place to heal from heartbreak — a place that was conducive to photography — and he discovered this house on Anderson Island.

We were only going to be friends. Now, we were both aware that somehow we needed to find a way to make this relationship work.

Sometimes you change your mind,
sometimes your mind changes you.

∞ ∞ ∞

Baggie Wallet

"**W**hat is that?" I snickered as I pointed toward his hand. His face flushed as he held up a sandwich baggie. The contents: money, his driver's license, and a credit card.

"I washed my wallet. I thought the microwave would dry it out quickly, but it curled the leather up into a hard ball. I didn't have time to buy another one." We both laughed. A great impression for his first trip to Oregon to visit me.

Though neither of us wanted, or expected, to get into a long-distance relationship, we agreed to a plan. If we wanted to make this work, we needed to find a way to see each other at least every other week, in spite of the 400 miles between us. Retirement afforded Sean a little more flexibility for travel. I still worked at the law firm but I had holidays, vacation, and personal days to use. That meant I could schedule four-day weekends to make a trip north once a month. We FaceTimed morning and evening. We sent text messages throughout the day. Having all this phone time enabled us to talk about everything under the sun; our interests, dislikes, financial habits, family dynamics, and even past relationships. I was grateful that I'd learned to communicate my feelings and opinions over the years and all this phone time opened opportunities to get even better with sharing.

Early October's warm air swirled around us as we drove along the winding country road with the convertible top down. Sean made his first trip to Oregon two weeks after we'd met, scheduling the trip over my birthday weekend. I could see the gleam in his eyes as the Miata hugged the curves. The look so familiar of a man in a fast car.

"Would you mind slowing down a little? There are a lot of accidents on this road." I clasped my hands together tightly to resist placing my hands on the dashboard to brace myself. I was familiar with this road. I knew he wasn't. He responded with a guilty smile, and slowed the car to a safer speed.

The pavement narrowed, then turned to gravel that crunched and shifted, throwing pebbles against the bottom of the car with a rhythmic popping noise.

We parked along the road, near the trailhead. Sean slung his SLR camera around his neck. His backpack was filled with our lunch, water, and sodas, ready for the two-mile hike to Rainie Falls. We stopped every five minutes to capture nature's beauty: views like the trickling streams of water that emerged from the hillside, crossed the trail, and cascaded down the cliff to the river below. The steep grade of the dirt path, riddled with rocks, tree roots, and puddles of water, posed dangerous conditions, making it necessary for every step to be careful and deliberate.

A cool gentle breeze rustled the autumn leaves making room for the shimmering sunlight to filter through, highlighting shades of gold, brown, and red. When we arrived at Rainie Falls, Sean sat on a boulder, camera to his eye, waiting — for that perfect shot of a salmon jumping out of the water, trying to reach the top of the falls. He finally succeeded. The misty spray of the falls dampened the rocks around us as we enjoyed the view and ate our lunch.

Me and Sean at Rainie Falls - October 2014.

On Sunday morning we strolled through Lithia Park and downtown Ashland, a college town 45 minutes southeast of Grants Pass. For lunch we stopped at a small pizza shop. That's where I spotted his baggie wallet.

We were driving back to Grants Pass when we heard a *thump thump thump* and the Miata began to wobble. Sean groaned. He steered the Miata to the side of the freeway, into the edge of a grassy field, away from the traffic speeding past us. He popped the trunk and removed the small spare and jack. His frustration mounted when, instead of raising the car, the jack plunged its way deeper into the soft ground with every pump of the handle.

"I have Triple-A. Let me call them to take care of it," I offered. Within the hour Triple-A had us back on the road. Sean seemed quieter on the drive back to Grants Pass. I sensed his stress. We decided to stop at the River's Edge Restaurant for an appetizer before heading to my house.

"We'd like an outside table with a river view, please." We ordered an appetizer and a margarita. "Salt on the rim for me, please," I told the waiter. The Rogue River is always a beautiful sight, even when it's in a raging winter state, but today it flowed gently, slapping the side of the bank and gurgling as it flowed over the rapids. The sounds were calming. A musician sat on a bar-stool close by and played soft music on his acoustic guitar. Sean relaxed as we laughed and shared stories. When we made our way to the door, Sean dropped a five spot in the guitarist's tip jar. It was something I discovered later that he always did — tip the musician. He is a musician and he understands the hard work and dedication that goes into the art.

Sean planned to leave early the next morning. He wanted to stop in the Portland area for a short visit with his son, before making his way north in time to catch the last ferry to the island. It was his son's birthday. Having to wait for Les Schwab's Tire Center to open gave him a later start than he'd hoped for. Sean called from the tire store,

"There's good news and bad," he said, with a bit of panic in his voice. "They fixed the tire for free because it was a Les Schwab tire, but I've lost my wallet."

Sean returned to my house to search for the missing baggie. He called the restaurant, knowing he had it in his hand when he tipped the musician. Nothing had been turned in. By now, Sean was definitely running late. The drive to Anderson Island takes seven hours. The last ferry would leave the dock at 8:30 pm. If he didn't leave soon, he wouldn't make it in time.

"I'll loan you $100 to get you home. You can take my credit

card for emergency use." A little embarrassed, he accepted my offer. My phone rang later that evening. Sean's voice sounded frazzled but relieved.

"I barely made it," he said. He had just boarded the ferry. "I didn't have time to stop and see Ben (his son)." He promptly returned my credit card and money by mail. Over the next few days his phone calls seemed short and the text messages dwindled. Then I received an email.

"A long-distance relationship may not be such a good idea. I'm not sure I want to make that trip on a regular basis. Let's stay friends."

"Just like that... an email, without even talking about it?" I shot back.

"You're right. We should talk." The trip had been a stressful disaster for him - a flat tire, a lost wallet, borrowing money to get home, rushing to catch the ferry, and missing his son's birthday. I agreed that we could still be friends, in lieu of a romantic relationship. I was disappointed but I mentally prepared myself for this outcome when I noticed his withdrawal. *Things happen for a reason. Maybe it's for the best.* I told myself. *After all, long-distance relationships are notoriously challenging.* I was familiar with the tempting road of self-pity, but I was determined not to take that path again.

Sean had previously invited me to attend his friend's wedding in late October. I chucked the idea at this point. The next week, Sean continued to text me daily. I responded, reminding myself not to read anything into it. Then he called to tell me the story:

"Since I didn't get to stop and see my son on my way home last week, I met him at a restaurant today. I gave him the birthday gift bag – the one I prepared for him at your house. He opened it and along with the birthday card, he pulled out a sandwich bag and asked 'What's this?' When I put the check in his bag, I must have dropped my baggie wallet in there too."

By this time, he had already replaced his credit card and driver's license. We laughed about the story, then he asked,

"Will you still come up for my friend's wedding?"

I did make the trip north and attended the weddings with him. The bride and groom had two ceremonies, each unique and special in its own way. The first was a traditional Vietnamese wedding, the second was a western wedding held the following day. This was my first time meeting this couple, and their families. They welcomed me with open arms, yet I awkwardly fidgeted as I tried to make small talk; uncomfortable attending such an intimate event of someone I didn't know.

After we'd stayed long enough to make a respectable showing at the reception, I urged Sean to leave. We walked hand in hand to the car. Sean wrapped his arms around me in a long embrace as we stood next to the car, then gave me a short gentle kiss. After I climbed into the passenger seat, Sean wedged his 5'10" — 205# body behind the wheel of his little Miata. I gave a sigh of relief as I felt the tension of the evening melting away. I fastened my seatbelt in the dim light. Sean put the key in the ignition. He paused,

"Oh, F___ it. I'm just gonna say it… I love you!"

At first glance, it may appear too hard.
Look again. Always look again.
Marianne Rodmacher

Ferry to Anderson Island. Mount Rainier
looks in the background.

∞ ∞ ∞

Baggy Jeans

I asked myself, *Is it Sean I'm attracted to or is it the magical romance of the island waterfront?* I didn't want my emotions being led down the wrong path this time, and I didn't want to go through another "opposites attract" situation either. After examining all aspects of our relationship, I realized both played into the equation. Yes, the island was magical, but more importantly, Sean and I had common interests and differences; there seemed to be an equal balance. I never got tired of his company whether we were together or talking on the phone, which we could do for hours.

"So what is it that keeps you interested in me?" I asked Sean. I knew what attracted me to him. I wanted to know why he had an interest in me.

"I was nervous about a relationship at first because I was shocked when my previous marriage ended. I was heartbroken and never wanted to go through such pain again. When I started falling for you, I paid close attention to the quality and longevity of the relationships in your life, and it was inspiring."

I asked what he meant by that.

"It seems everybody who has been part of your life adores you — even your ex-daughters-in-law are still a part of your life. And the fact that you have worked for the same boss for 20 plus years speaks volumes about your character. I decided this relationship is one I can trust."

I felt thankful that one of the greatest things about our relationship was that we could communicate.

With all the phone calls, text messages, and discussing nearly every possible subject, there was one silly subject I didn't bring up. I kept the baggy jeans opinion to myself. Robbie became the recipient of my story as we settled ourselves in the front seat of her jeep.

"He's so cute but I wish he would wear a little tighter pants instead of those baggy jeans!" Like little girls sharing secrets, we giggled as I latched my seatbelt. I'd placed my phone on my lap to do so. Then panic struck!

"Oh my gosh! What did I just say?" I asked. "Whatever it was, it went to Sean as a voice text!" My phone indicated an audio message had been delivered successfully.

"What?" Robbie's response was nearly as dramatic as mine. We stared at each other wide-eyed, then we broke out in uncontrollable laughter. Tears of hysteria trickled down our cheeks. We knew what we'd been talking about – and now we'd been caught. I'd have to face the embarrassing consequences when Sean listened to the message.

"What are you gonna do?" Robbie asked. I took a deep breath and looked at my phone again.

"OK, wait!" my chest quivered as I gasped with relief. "The audio text is only a few seconds long. He couldn't have heard the entire conversation!" About five minutes later my phone pinged.

"You wish... what??" That was all he received..."I wish." We were off the hook! I sent a brief reply.

"*Opps*, sorry you got that. Not meant for you." I admitted the entire conversation to him at a much later date. The tight jeans became a running joke between us. Then one day he made a mistake.

"I'll tell you what. If we ever get married, you can dress me any way you want — but until then I'm going to keep wearing my comfy Costco jeans."

Love doesn't erase the past, but it makes the future different.

∞∞∞

Chapter Seventeen

An Agate, An Email and a Name

"Did you find an agate?" I asked, feeling a little annoyed. I'd been unsuccessful in my search for agates today and now he finds one right under my feet.

The narrow dirt path to Carlson Cove, our favorite hike on the island, led us through a wall of salal, salmonberry shrubs and evergreen trees. The dirt trail, classified easy to medium, ended at the cusp of a cliff and a flight of steps leading down to a bridge. The wooden planks creaked as we walked across the lagoon's makeshift bridge. It touched the top of the water, rising and falling with the tide. Sean anticipated a radiant sunset so he brought his camera to capture some photographs.

We arrived early and searched the shore for agates. The sun dipped in the sky, bathing the beach, lagoon and hillside with a soft golden hue. Those evening rays often reflected the translucent areas of the agate, making them easier for me to spot, though not today. Agates or not, a day on this beach could never be a bad day. Each trip guaranteed a sighting of kingfishers darting about, chattering to one another, dipping low to catch the evening insects that hovered above the lagoon. Pigeon Guillemots flew in and out of small holes in the cliff side where they nested. And, my favorite, the great blue heron, fished off the shoreline. If startled, their gigantic wing span carried them gracefully over the water, their long legs dangling below them, to a place where they felt safe from us. There, they would set themselves back down, and again scour the water for fish. Most of our trips to this beach meant sharing with wildlife and no one else. Peaceful, calm.

The golden hour is a photographer's delight, and now it seemed to help him find the agate I searched for. Expecting him to hold up a beauty, I prepared a jealous courtesy smile to support his find. Instead, he asked,

"Will you marry me?" Taken by surprise, I hesitated, then responded with the first thing that came to mind.

"Do you promise it will be forever?"

"Yes."

"Then absolutely."

We hugged, kissed and posed for our first engagement selfie. I went back to searching for agates while Sean's camera lens clicked nonstop, capturing the kaleidoscope of rapidly changing red, pink, orange and blue colors filling the sky as the sun lowered to the horizon. I'd become accustomed to Sean's camera addiction for nature and accustomed to the camera aimed in my direction.

"Es-ther — Es-ther!" I heard him shouting from a distance. I looked up and struck a pose for him. He waved as if swatting at a fly. "Will you move over? You're blocking the sunset!"

Shaking my head in disbelief, I reluctantly moved on down the beach, out of his camera view.

———

I called each of my sons on my drive home to Oregon to inform them of the engagement. Duane's children immediately named him Grandpa Sean. Concerned that my family may have some reservations about our getting engaged in a short, three-month timeframe, Sean sent an email to all four of my sons:

"I know you probably think our engagement is quick. If we were in our thirties, I'd agree. But, at our ages, we have learned through experience what we want and don't want in a person. We've spent more time talking with each other via FaceTime and text messages than most people would have spent talking if they'd been going on dates."

Sean received the following reply from my son, Stephen, and shared it with me.

"Sean, I got your email. Thank you. I just want to remind you; my mother has four sons. One who can infect you with biochemicals (he works for a biotech company), one who can karate chop you (he's a 4th degree black belt in martial arts), one who can dig a hole and bury you (he owns an excavation company) and one who can cover it up (he's a politician) and also send you straight to Hell (because he's also a pastor)! So, congratulations — and welcome to the family!"

"And that was my shy son!" I told him. Sean shared that story at our wedding, and in many conversations since.

"That's how guys bond." He said, a proud smile on his face. In his eyes, he and Stephen had now bonded.

"You're lucky. You should have seen what they did to Sam, another guy I dated." I told Sean the story:

Sam flew down from Spokane to visit me and I took him

259

to Stephen's house for dinner on Thanksgiving Day. Duane's family was there. As we drove in, I noticed a noose hanging from the front porch rafters. A pick and shovel stood next to the door. I knocked and Stephen answered the door. The living room was dark except for a light at the far end of the room. I introduced Sam. Stephen shook his hand and said, "Follow me." We walked through the dim light and Stephen motioned to a chair and told Sam to sit there.

"This is my brother, Duane." Duane sat across the table from Sam, behind a bright light that now shone on Sam's face.

"We have some questions for you." Duane spoke in a gruff, interrogative voice.

"Ok. I've got answers, I think," my date answered, a little meek but going along with the facade.

"How do you feel about abstinence?" Duane asked.

"Well, I only drink a glass of wine now and then," came the answer.

A roar of laughter came from the family members who were sitting nearby in the dark.

"Oh my gosh! I can't believe they are doing that to him! ... Oh, wait, ...yes, I can!" my daughter-in-law, René, said once she regained her composure. We all had a good laugh and enjoyed dinner. As we prepared to leave, Duane leaned toward my date and spoke quietly, but purposely loud enough for me to hear.

"I'm sorry things didn't work out between you and my mom!" he winked at me.

"Does he know something I don't know?" Sam asked. He

laughed and gave me a hug. He never went with me to my son's house again.

———

Being a career journalist, Sean is a word guy. I assumed he pronounced my name with a lisp — Es-THER — to tease me. Esther is an old name that is seldom heard with our generation. I thought I was named after my mother's best friend, Esther Dennison, who came to visit us once a year. On the same trip I made to Washington when I met Sean, I thumbed through my sister's photo albums. There was a picture of a woman titled, Aunt Esther.

"I didn't know we had an Aunt Esther," I told Phyllis.

"Who do you think you were named after?" she asked. I'd always thought I was named after my mother's friend. It wasn't until I was 63 years old that I realized my namesake. Until I was an adult, I never met another Esther my age or younger. Those I'd met were a generation older. I've since met several younger Esthers.

I never asked Sean about the odd pronunciation of my name until we'd been engaged for a few months. I just figured I'd humor him by staying quiet, allowing him the fun he seemed to be having with it. Finally, one day I commented.

"You crack me up the way you pronounce my name." We were talking on the phone when I mentioned the subject.

"What do you mean?" His oblivion to the comment surprised me.

"You pronounce it Es-THer."

"Well, how do you pronounce it?"

"It's Est - her."

"But it has a th in it," he objected. He sounded dubious of my correcting him. That evening, I received a googled audio message:

"E-S-T-H-E-R is pronounced as Est-her," the robotic voice said. A text under the message stated,

"You're right!"

"After 64 years, do you really think I don't know how to pronounce my own name?" I typed in response.

Building confidence will mean turning my doubts and my misgivings of myself into positive thoughts. Believing in myself — one step at a time.

———

The Stark Family - November 2014
Larry, Stephen, me, Duane and Chris

∞∞∞

Faith and Trust

"There's one thing I'm a little nervous about, Mom." My son spoke to me in private. "You're retiring from your job, moving away from family and friends, getting married, and relocating to a small remote island, all at once."

I understood his concerns although I felt confident in my decision. — *Me? Confident? What a change!* — The two concerns I had were: (1) By now I'd become very independent. With 19 years of being single, I was accountable only to myself (and my adult children, of course). I wondered if I could adjust that attitude. I had full control of my life as a single woman. I'd have to work on the control issue. (2) My main concern arose when I discovered Sean was a nonbeliever. I'd told myself if I ever married again, it would be to a Christian of strong faith. Since I rededicated my life, my faith has remained an important part of my life. Sean and I seemed equally yoked in most other areas. I talked with my son, Duane, since he was a pastor, about Sean's lack of a Christian faith.

"Well, Mom, if you have problems, you won't have a husband who will pray through the problem with you."

"But I've never had that anyway."

The following Sunday, after talking with Duane about the subject, I attended Applegate Christian Fellowship. The pastor's words spoke directly to me:

"When we encounter a non-believer, all we can do is be a good witness and pray for them. We can't manipulate them into believing."

I decided to talk with Sean about it. At this point I felt especially grateful Sean and I were able to talk openly with each other.

"I have one concern about us, and that is our difference in faith. I'm a strong believer, and you say you're a nonbeliever," I told him. "One thing that would definitely be a problem in our relationship is if you started criticizing my faith."

"Why would I do that?" he asked.

"Because most non-believers criticize those who believe."

"I would never do that," he promised. We reached an agreement: he wouldn't try to discourage my faith; I wouldn't try to manipulate him into believing. Early in our relationship I had told Sean:

"I cringe when I hear people use the F word. I just don't like it!"

He had a tendency to use the word when he wanted to emphasize something. He assured me he would no longer use it around me. He later confessed,

"I thought I'd stop using the word around you, but I realized it doesn't work that way. I had to stop using it altogether." — and he did.

Faith is believing in something
when common sense tells you not to.

∞ ∞ ∞

Words of Affirmation

I attribute the longevity of 26 years as a legal assistant for my boss, Richard Adams, to his ability to make me feel valued. He often attached notes to files that read:

"Great job, you should have been the attorney on this one." I once received an email from him: "Have I mentioned lately that I appreciate all you do here in the office?" His words validated my worth as an employee.

The Five Love Languages, by Gary Chapman, has been instrumental in understanding myself and others around me, specifically Sean. Most people have a mixture of all five languages, with one primary love language.

Words of Affirmation
Quality Time
Acts of Service
Physical Touch
Gifts

Mine? No doubt, Words of Affirmation. When I hear encouragement, compliments, or praise, I feel loved, or at least appreciated. Those words of affirmation build my confidence, fill my love tank. That probably relates to my spiritual gift being encouragement to others.

During a phone call with Sean, I mentioned the book to him. I was delighted he had read the book and pleased to discover his love language was also words of affirmation. Lowest on the list for both of us is gifts. We agree gifts are nice but are not an important factor in our lives. Sharing the same love languages makes it much easier to fill the other's love tank.

Some people can't believe in themselves
until they know someone else believes in them first.

∞∞∞

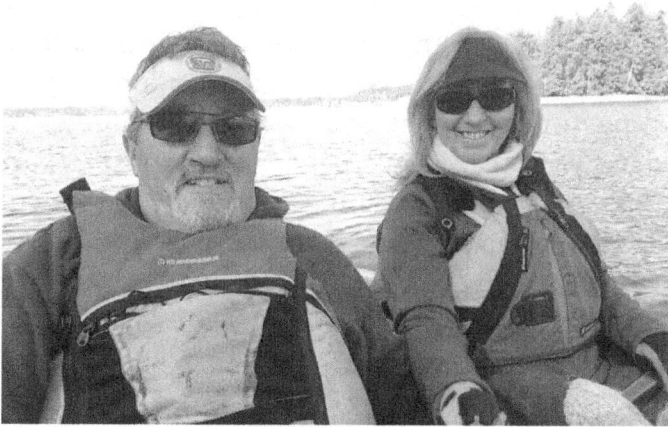

Sean and me kayaking
in Balch Passage.

∞∞∞

Chapater Eighteen

Promises & Vows

"**S**ean and Esther, I pronounce you husband and wife." Sherry Nelson, Sean's friend and our ordained pastor, chuckled before she continued, "You may now update your Facebook page." The guests roared with laughter as Sean pulled out his iPhone. We turned to face the guests as I leaned my head toward his and he snapped a picture. Our first selfie as husband and wife.

"Now... you may kiss the bride."

The rhythmic beat of *Louie Louie* thundered through the loudspeakers. Hand in hand Sean and I skipped, twirled and danced down the dry grassy aisle, past our family and friends, who were now standing, cheering, clapping. The wedding felt... What's the word? — *magical*. Not once did I feel nervous or doubtful that I'd made the right decision. The unrestrained smile on my face sparkled with happiness. The strapless, street length white dress, covered with lace, was stunning against my summer tan, creating the epitome of a lovely bride. Sean looked handsome in his white slacks and purple dress shirt. Pete Cammon's apple orchard provided a relaxed and casual setting for the wedding. Our choice of upbeat music got guests on their feet doing a Conga line dance and the YMCA dance. We had one little snafu during the ceremony – but what is a wedding without a fun story or two making it interesting? My maid of honor, Robbie, forgot her bouquet when she walked the aisle with Mike Trygstad, Sean's best man. No big deal. I doubt anyone noticed — except my son, Larry, as he prepared to walk with me. As the bride's music played, and we took a step forward, Larry glanced toward the gazebo where we had been gathered. He spotted the bouquet on the metal chair, ran over, grabbed it, and held it behind his back as we embarked on our walk down the aisle. He handed me off to Sean and after a hug, made a pass in front of the altar and discreetly handed Robbie the bouquet.

———

When we got engaged, we intended to have a small ceremony on the deck of our home overlooking Puget Sound, a quaint gathering of family and a few close friends. But, it didn't turn out that way. Once the engagement became public on the island, the invitation list grew to an approximate count of 150 people.

"Getting married on the island is a big thing," friends told Sean. "Finding love in your retirement years is something to celebrate and this community will want to celebrate with you."

With that in mind, we moved the venue – to our neighbor's beautiful green orchard, amongst the apple trees. The space was big enough to accommodate a large group. Sean had lived on the island for two years. Each visit I made to the island, he introduced me to one – or a half dozen – new faces. I'd only become well acquainted with a handful. Since this would be my home community, I welcomed the idea of a larger gathering.

Sean edited photographs on his computer as he ate his breakfast at the cafe, a morning ritual of his since the cafe had better internet service than at home. During his morning meal, Katrina Wiggins approached him.

"Hi, I'm Katrina. I hear you're getting married. I'm going to be your wedding coordinator." Seeing Sean's surprise at the bold comment by this woman he barely recognized, she continued, "Don't worry. It won't cost you anything. It's just what I do." Sean had no idea how I would react to our newly appointed wedding coordinator, but he told Katrina Wiggins what little he knew about the wedding plan, indicating we were planning to barbecue chicken skewers for our reception.

"Waldo, come here." Katrina motioned for Mike Walentiny to join them. "Put July 25th on your calendar. You're going to be barbecuing chicken that day for Sean's wedding." I personally had never met Mike (aka Waldo), nor his wife, Shirley, until they showed up on our wedding day, ready to cook the skewers we had waiting for them. I later became very well acquainted with this amazing woman, Shirley Hughes, with whom I shared an interest in art.

Sean explained to me the conversation with Katrina. I planned to retire from my job at the law firm on June 30th. Our wedding was set for July 25th. Since I would be planning the wedding from Oregon, it made sense. Katrina knew nearly everyone on the island. I agreed with the plan. My next trip to the island, I met with Katrina and a handful of others she solicited to help. Wedding ideas were tossed about.

"We want to keep it simple and inexpensive. This isn't a first marriage for either of us," I told them.

Pete Cammon, our next-door neighbor, volunteered to grow purple and white petunias in her garden which should be in full bloom by the July wedding date. The flowers would match my color scheme. Another lady volunteered the use of mason jars for bouquets to garnish the tables.

"We'll make it potluck style. Potlucks are popular on the island." Katrina said. "Everyone will love it." Islanders always joked that "you can't throw a rock without hitting a potluck."

As our July wedding date approached, the lush green orchard faded to yellow and brown with the summer heat. Too late to change venues, I forced a smile, trying to curb my attitude.

"Instead of a lovely green lawn, guess we're gonna have a field of straw." I shared my disappointment with Katrina.

"It's going to be so beautiful nobody will even notice." Katrina assured.

Katrina was right. Her large white wedding canopy shaded long tables covered with white linens. Pete's elegant purple and white flowers were interlaced throughout the variety of food. White chairs were placed at linen covered tables where guests sat during the ceremony. Each table held a mason jar bouquet of purple and white petunias, plastic cups, and a bottle of wine for a toast to the bride and groom. The straw-like grass was neatly mowed, barely noticeable under the rows of white chairs and tables.

It is nine years later as I write this story. Sean and I strive to live by the vows we made to each other on July 25, 2015.

Sean:
On this day, I offer you my hand, my heart, my promise, that I will walk with you, faithfully, courageously, hilariously, hand in hand, wherever our journey leads us, living, learning, loving, together, for all the days of our lives.

Esther:
I accept the hand, the heart, and the promise you offer. In return, I promise you will never regret the choice you have

made today. I want to add to your life, not take anything away. I will laugh with you and cry with you, I will learn from you, and I'll teach you. I promise to be your biggest fan... and your toughest critic. My love will be shown to you daily... and my goal is that we will never forget... what made us fall in love in the first place.

Larry was nominated by his brothers to speak on their behalf at our wedding reception.

"I can tell how much islanders have come to love Sean, but for many of the islanders, this wedding is your introduction to our mom. So the one thing my brothers and I agree you should know about her is — our mom is all heart."

His heartwarming speech brought tears to my eyes. Then Sean and I laughed at his closing statement.

"We can't believe our mother fell in love with a man who loves karaoke!"

Find the confidence in whatever way you can to just
keep moving on to the next stage in life.

∞ ∞ ∞

Larry carries Robbie's bouquet behind his
back as he walks me down the aisle.

∞∞∞

∞∞∞

Me and Sean
First selfie as husband and wife.

∞ ∞ ∞

Me - Sherry Nelson, officiating - Sean

∞∞∞

Karaoke Virgin

I t didn't take long to learn of Sean's passion after we started dating: singing karaoke. A visit to the island never went without karaoke singing. Sean had a small karaoke CD machine that projected the words on his television. His collection of discs held more than a 1,000 song choices. At first, I listened – never willing to attempt to sing. I was much too shy for that. Over time, I timidly joined him with a quiet, almost inaudible voice. Four years of high school chorus classes had me quietly singing alto next to others, never a soloist. Sean never missed the karaoke nights held monthly at the Lakeshore Restaurant.

Sean chose an Alaskan cruise for our honeymoon. A first-time cruise for both of us. When I noticed karaoke would be held nightly in one of the clubs, I was convinced that karaoke played a major role in his choosing this particular ship. After a night or two in the club, I realized Sean wasn't the only karaoke addict on the cruise – Rick and Debbie, a couple from Texas, were also in attendance every night. Rick moonlighted as an impersonator, singing at clubs. If he sang a Randy Travis song, you'd swear Randy Travis was in the room. Debbie sang right on pitch with her country music. After attending the early theater show, we'd head to the club. It wasn't uncommon for the club to be empty, other than the four of us and the karaoke jockey, for a large portion of the night. Sean, Debbie and Rick coaxed me to sing.

"This would be the perfect time, Esther. There's just the four of us." Debbie pleaded. My chest tightened with the heaviness of desire - the desire to get on that stage and sing. They continued to coax. I squirmed in my bar stool. I timidly licked the salt from the rim of my margarita glass — wishing I had the courage to get up there and sing.

"Maybe after one more margarita," I said, doubtful it would actually happen. I fidgeted with my napkin, damp from the condensation off my glass.

"Oh honey, forget the margarita and all those extra calories. Go for the straight shot!" Debbie ordered a shot of Tequila. "Now go for it."

I downed the Tequila, chased it with a swig of water and continued nervously fidgeting with my napkin. An instant of courage hit me and I wrote "Patsy Cline, I Fall to Pieces" on a song slip. Debbie snatched it from my hand and took it to the karaoke jockey before I could change my mind. With only four of us in the club, he immediately called my name.

My stomach churned. *You can do this, Esther,* I tried to encourage myself. My three comrades cheered me on as I walked to the stage. My body trembled as my hands clutched the microphone tight. *I hope my shaking won't be visible from their table! I need to relax!* I loosened my grip, turned my face from the microphone and cleared my throat. My jaw quivered as I began to sing. The words flowed from my lips. I was pleased to be in tune, despite the tension in my voice. *Relax Esther!* I took deeper breaths as I sang… it helped. Then, it happened – a show must have ended. A large group of people poured into the club – right in the middle of my song! I wanted to stop right then! But I didn't. I continued with the song.

To my surprise, a lot of the couples went directly to the dance floor, swaying to the tune of my voice — or maybe just to the tune of the music. It's a compliment to a singer when someone dances as you sing. My body trembled as I walked back to the table, this time with excitement that I actually did it — and because I received a big applause from the crowd.

"You did great!" Debbie said as she gave me a big hug! *Well I don't know about great,* I thought, *but I got up there!*

"Your eyes got so big when people walked in," Sean said. "You looked like a deer caught in the headlights." he laughed as he hugged me.

I didn't summon the courage to try it a second time during our cruise, but the ice had been broken – I was no longer a karaoke virgin.

Our honeymoon was extended to a trip to Grants Pass for an Oregon reception and a jet boat dinner trip on the Rogue River. When we arrived back on the island, we settled into a life together. I recalled the innocent comment Sean made during our early days of dating, "If we ever get married, you can dress me any way you want." Within two weeks of returning, Sean's baggy Costco jeans found their way to the Goodwill bin — the corduroy pants joined them some months later. New clothes hung in his closet.

————

Though the ice had been broken on the cruise ship, my island debut didn't go as well. I agreed to sing at the Lakeshore Restaurant if Sean sang a duet with me. Of course he agreed. Sean never turns down an opportunity to sing. We practiced over and over at home, *I've Got You Babe,* by Sonny & Cher, an old standby for newbie singers, I later discovered. I knew all the words. I'd memorized them in my high school days. Nerves can do strange things to a person. The music began and my mind went blank — even with the words on the monitor in front of us. I waited for Sean to begin singing. He didn't; he curiously watched me. The music continued playing, people watched and waited, then I realized the opening verse was mine. Half way through the first verse we finally got on track. I shook my head in disbelief as we returned to our table, feeling mortified at the performance. In spite of my humility, we laughed and joked about it, as my brain secretly screamed, *What a spectacle!*

"I'll do better next time," I assured Sean, thinking to myself, *IF there is a next time!* Sean didn't seem bothered by the failed performance.

I sang more at home but balked when asked to sing in public. Sean invited friends to come over to the house for karaoke parties. Then, while at the Lakeshore one night, Eddie came to our table.

"Esther, it's time for you to get up there and sing. I see you singing along with all the songs while you sit here," he said.

Kim and Eddie were the island karaoke jockeys. They were as faithful as Sean, encouraging me every month while I sat and listened to others. Eventually I succumbed to the coaxing and sang my first solo – Sammi Smith's, *Help Me Make it Through the Night*. I trembled but it otherwise went well. I began singing more and more, ignoring the twisting knot in my stomach. My courage came by telling myself, *I can do just as good as that person!* Sometimes I did, sometimes I didn't.

"I love having a wife I can sing with," Sean delighted in telling people. Then he'd add, "Now, when I want to sing, I have to pry the microphone out of her fingers."

You have two choices: Your commitment, or your fear.

279

Island Life

"The power's out and we've nothing to do. Want to play a game?" Sean phoned our friends, Sally and Bruce Buchanan, who lived a quarter mile away. Power outages were common on the densely forested island. Wind or heavy snow frequently brought power lines to the ground.

"Sure, come on over." Sally said. The roads were packed from a week of heavy snow, passable only with 4x4 vehicles. Anderson Island ranked low on the priority list when it came to Pierce County sending snow plows across the ferry to clear the roads. Many residents were stranded, unable to get out of their driveways. Tire tracks created by 4x4 vehicles melted into deep ruts.

With a go ahead from Sally, Sean and I slipped into our snow pants, then strapped on our snowshoes and headlamps. Dark clouds hung low in the sky as if teasing, ready to open up, dusting the ground with another layer of white. The icy air tingled my cheeks and nose as we trekked over the dirty-white road, scattered with pine needles.

We gathered around a small table in front of the wood stove when we reached the Buchannan's house. Its crackling fire warming us. We spread the Rummikub tiles over the table top and played the game by the light of our headlamps, still strapped to our heads.

Snowshoe trek to the
Buchanan house.

Since power outages happened frequently during winter months, we learned to turn them into adventures. We lit candles and Sean would play his guitar or we'd practice our ukuleles.

On another blackout night, we invited Bill and Lorena McPhail to our house for a game. Our wood burning earth stove kept our house warm while others who used electric heat struggled with the cold during the outages. The island's community center had a generator and also invited those with no heat to hang out at the center. The McPhails arrived, the candles were lit, Rummikub tiles lay spread out over the table, and we sat down to play. The power came back on.

"Well, that's no fun," Sean said. We all shrugged and laughed.

"Let's turn the lights off and play anyway." I suggested. That's what we did.

Power outage game night
with the McPhails.

∞ ∞ ∞

Living for years in Oregon, where winters included snow, ice, lots of rain, and gray skies, I envied retirees who spent their winters in warmer locations. When I retired and married Sean, the idea of snowbirding resurfaced in my mind. I mentioned it to Sean.

"Let's try it out with a vacation before we commit to an entire winter." Sean suggested.

We rented Debbie Coleman's second bedroom in Scottsdale, Arizona for two weeks. The arrangement worked well. We spent the days entertaining ourselves in Arizona's warm winter temperature; mornings we hiked and afternoons we enjoyed the swimming pool, conveniently located across the street from Debbie's condo.

The following year we spent two weeks in Mesa, Arizona. On 10 of those days we laced up our hiking boots and set out to conquer the trails in the Phoenix area. Our favorite was the climb to Weaver's Needle on the Peralta Trail. Our hikes take longer than the typical hiker. Sean makes frequent stops to capture the flora and fauna along the way. This hike was extremely rewarding for a photographer. The steep inclines and declines of the rocky terrain is a showcase for Arizona's iconic cactus: the stately saguaro; a slow-growing cactus that can take 10 years to grow one inch and starts to develop branches between ages 50-70. They reach their full height, approximately 45 feet, around 200 years old. The other cactus of interest was the teddy bear cholla, whose stem is almost completely obscured by its silvery-white, fuzzy looking spines. I kept plenty of distance between me and the teddy bear, and its sharp needles.

Other hikes included an intermediate trail through the Superstition Mountains, and a gentle uphill climb in the White Tank Mountains.

Each year we extended the Arizona experience a little longer. The third year we rented Debbie's condo for a month while she was out of town. Sunny skies, even for a short time, revitalized me after days and weeks of gray skies and rain in the Pacific Northwest.

The large windows in our Anderson Island living room, and the deck that overlooked Puget Sound and Eagle Island, provided us with a year-round theater of nature. Each season brought a new source of sounds. I often woke to the faint, redundant droning sound of the tugboat, Danielle, as she pulled a log raft, her consistent hum whispering, *I think I can, I think I can.* as she chugged through Balch Passage. When she neared Eagle Island, the harbor seals, who hitched rides on the logs, would dive off the logs and into the water, making their way to the shoreline to sunbathe.

Splashing water, grunts, groans and throaty growls can be heard throughout the night during the breeding season of harbor seals, who mate in the water. Late July babies are born on the shoreline of Eagle Island. Mamas usher their seal pups into the water as soon as possible. Bald eagles swoop down and clean up the birthing mess, leaving the shore clean before the incoming tide can wash away their easy source of food.

Canada geese use Eagle Island as a nesting ground. Their honking was a familiar, frequent sound. The crested cormorant is a large black bird often seen perched on pilings with its wide wing-span stretched out. The name is derived from sea raven. Their snorts resemble that of a pig as they roost in the nearby trees.

Summer weather brings boats of every kind to Balch Passage. Sean and I often kayaked Balch Passage during slack tide. We could paddle the same area and see something different each time: mama harbor seals barked warning to their pups to stay away from us; an osprey swooping out of the sky, crashing into the water, rising with a fish; a blue heron squawking as its six-foot wingspan gracefully carries it overhead in a near slow-motion movement; and a seagull carrying a clam shell over a rocky beach and dropping it. It repeated the process over and over until the shell shattered and the gull could retrieve its meal. When the sky is clear, the majestic Mount Rainier looms high over the horizon.

Three consecutive years we paddled the circumference of the island, a seven-hour excursion for us. We paid close attention to the tide table so we spent only a short time paddling against the tide.

There is one bear who swims from the mainland to the island annually, feasting on huckleberries and salmonberries. He makes his way through the island's orchards, scrounging the fallen apples. An abundance of deer inhabit the island and are treated as pets, fed from the hand. The large population of coyotes are treated as villains, with residents fearful for their small fur babies.

With the daily J-O-B out of the way, the hours in a day seemed to have increased, giving time to explore new interests: walking became a daily exercise for me; Sean and I learned to play pickleball; and the guitar I'd stored in my closet for years came out of hiding. With Sean as my teacher, I learned enough chords to play a variety of songs. A year later I switched from guitar to ukulele.

I appreciate the time retirement has given me. I discovered an entirely new world – once I learned to put fears behind me and open opportunity's door.

If you want to live a life you've never lived, you
have to do things you've never done.

∞∞∞

Chapter Nineteen

Paint with Esther

"You should consider teaching paint-and-sip classes." I flushed, feeling a slight adrenaline spike at Aysin's suggestion.

"I couldn't teach others." I meekly shook my head. The thought hadn't crossed my mind. I'd only been painting for a matter of months. *Or could I?* I daringly entertained the idea for an instant. I became a wanna-be artist a year earlier. *It will be something new to try*, I thought.

Like many small locations, Anderson Island has a sizable community of artists. In 2016, a drawing class was being offered and I prompted Sean to sign up with me. It didn't take long to discover drawing was not my calling — or Sean's.

My next attempt: watercolors. Sean decided to leave the artistry idea to me and opted out. I couldn't leave the painting alone and multiple attempts to fix a watercolor turned into a muddy mess. Oil painting – not enough patience. The drying time was too long for my project-oriented brain. I became frustrated and reluctantly gave up on art.

Winter set in and dark, dreary clouds, pouring rain, and frequent power outages kept us indoors. My thoughts returned to the lingering desire to discover an artistic side of me. I recalled my daughter-in-law, Dusti, painting with acrylics. I found an inexpensive starter kit on Amazon. *It's worth a try.*

While I anxiously waited for the supplies to arrive, I watched YouTube tutorials. I started a playlist where I saved the videos I wanted to try. When the package arrived, I tore into it, eager to get started. I had already set up my paint station. Rather than using an extra bedroom upstairs, I placed a table near the glass doors leading to the deck. I know that when I'm excited about something, I sometimes obsess, spending hours at a time on the project. By placing my art station in our large living room, I could still be near Sean. I would paint while he watches movies on television. My journey to become an artist set sail.

I painted for hours following tutorials. I searched online for reference photos to embellish, creating my own versions. As with everything I do, Sean became my number one fan and encourager.

"Those are good. Why don't you post a picture of it on Facebook?" Though I was pleased with my early progress, I was sensitive to the possibility of negative feedback. I was afraid that a troll — someone who relishes in saying disrespectful things on people's posts — might respond. If that happened, it would destroy any painting confidence I'd built up at this point. I resisted the urge to brag.

I had been painting 14 consecutive days when I completed an 8"x10" canvas I named *The Fashion Hat Woman.* My enthusiasm was obvious when I showed it to Sean that evening. It didn't take much for him to persuade me this time. I opened Facebook, uploaded the picture and typed a comment, "Today's painting, *The Fashion Hat Woman.*" I sat nervously. *Should I post it or not?* I still feared negative feedback. *But this one's pretty good.* I decided to take the risk. I clicked the "post" button. The next morning I received a message.

"Is this painting for sale, Esther? I'd love to buy it!" Clayton Peterson, an islander I had not yet met, purchased the painting for $50. I walked on Cloud 9 that day – it was a pretty exhilarating feeling.

Labor Day's Art in the Park boosted my morale further. I set up a booth next to Sean's. He sold matted and framed island photographs and his Anderson Island calendar. I had a large variety of landscape and impressionistic canvases I painted the previous six months. I entered several paintings in the art contest. My *Moonlight over Mount Rainier* won the People's Choice Award. and it sold! I sold a handful of other paintings including *Multnomah Falls in Autumn,* one of my favorite 16"x20" framed canvases. It went for $250.

Then came that pivotal moment — a suggestion that altered my path as an artist. Aysin Clay suggested I teach painting classes. She was referring to paint-and-sip style classes, where a group of attendees enjoy a snack, a glass of wine, and paint a specific subject in a set period of time.

"I love your style and I'm sure your classes will be full." Aysin continued to encourage me. "Will you think about it?" I told her I'd consider it, doubtful I would take that step — a bit out of my comfort range. As the week went by, I kept thinking about it. *It would be fun to do — I think.* Of course, Sean encouraged me. After further discussing the possibility with Aysin, I scheduled a class for the following month — time to order supplies, and time to work up the needed courage. Word spread quickly on our small island and the class was filled in short order. A limit of nine students fit comfortably in my dining room.

In the meantime, I received a call from Patricia. She worked as an activity director at a women's dementia center. She wanted to know what I'd charge to teach a class of ten ladies with different levels of dementia.

"I'll do the class for free, if I can use my refurbished canvases." I could repaint the canvases white to reuse them.

"That would be awesome," she said. "They won't know the difference if they are used or new canvases."

We set a date prior to the class I scheduled on the island. This would give me hands-on experience of teaching.

Sean and Patricia assisted me with that class, refilling water tubs and encouraging the ladies. One woman's eyes beamed as she showed how she meticulously painted my new wooden easel.

"Does this look ok?" another woman asked while stirring her paint around on the paper plate we used as a palette.

"It looks beautiful," I assured her. "Now would you like to put some of that paint on the canvas too?"

Another lady sat quietly, her head tilted down, looking rather shy. I wandered over to check her canvas. It remained clean, as did her brushes.

"Would you like me to help you get started?" I gently suggested, picking up a brush.

"No!" She shuddered as she shook her head fiercely. "I don't want anything to do with that!" She pulled back as she pointed to the plate of paint. "I already tried it," she said. "It tastes terrible!" She scowled, then stuck out her red, paint stained tongue.

These precious ladies taught me something I needed to know. *I can teach a painting class, and I would enjoy it.*

My island class was a huge success and I launched "Paint with Esther." I filled three to four monthly classes in addition to private parties scheduled by groups of close friends, and private parties for families.

My art career flourished because I took a risk and ignored that nagging fear — *What if I fail?*

My paintings have won a wide range of ribbons at art shows and county fairs from Grand Champion, Most Visual, and People's Choice, to First, Second and Third place. I've sold paintings at craft fairs, online, and I've been commissioned for specific paintings.

"I'd love to take your class, Esther, but I can't even draw stick people." That's one comment I frequently hear when I offer painting classes. I always have the same response:

"That's ok because we're not going to be painting stick people."

There are times when I consider ending the teaching portion of my career. Then I recall the smiles when a student realizes they really can paint something that looks similar to the reference photo. Students meet new faces and cultivate new friends within our small group classes. It takes me back to my earlier days when I realized my gifts were hospitality and encouragement. I love bringing joy to others.

My jazz player painting was on the
cover of *The Islander* magazine in 2019.

———

My 16"x20" black & white wolf painting.

∞ ∞ ∞

It's Just a Game - Or is it??

The stadium rumbled; *Stomp stomp, clap clap, stomp stomp, clap clap.* My eardrums vibrate from the deafening roar of the cheering fans. The batter approaches the box. The pitcher nods his head, lifts his knee, and winds up to throw the ball. The crowd is silent for a split second — then a loud *CRACK* brings bellowing cheers, high fives, jumping, hugging – even with strangers who sat nearby. That familiar *CRACK* resonating through the air left no doubt the ball would travel out of the ballpark. The scoreboard changed, 6 - 5. Mariners take the win. Those exhilarating moments, whether I'm in the stands experiencing the game in person, or sitting at home watching on TV, is what keeps me an avid baseball fan.

I've been a Mariners fan for over 20 years; since my son moved to the Seattle area after graduating from college. When I visit Larry, an afternoon at the ballpark to watch a Mariners game is usually on the schedule. My addiction to baseball goes back even further. I recall my mother watching the World Series on television each year. Duane and Chris played minor and major league baseball. Chris, at age 10, hit a home run out of the ballpark in the first little league game he ever played. In 1991, Duane played with the 13-year-old Babe Ruth baseball league. His all-star team made it to the Little League World Series. Their team placed fifth in the nation. John and I followed that team to district, then to Wyoming for Regionals. Because I had to return to work, we were unable to make the trip to New Jersey to watch their World Series games. I listened to the broadcast on KAJO radio while I worked. The local radio station was proud to air such an exciting event for the youth of our community.

My grandson Nicholas played little league baseball and I was an avid spectator. His interest expanded to other sports as high school approached. He decided to go out for track. I knew the seasons overlapped. Chris and Duane both made the same decision at that age.

"How are you going to juggle the two sports?" My eyebrow raised as I questioned him. Sean loved to tease me about how I raised my eyebrows when I wanted to make a statement. My head tilted as I shot Nicholas the evil eye, indicating he should give me the answer I wanted to hear, yet suspicious as to what his answer might be.

"I'm not playing baseball this year Grandma."

"What?" My voice and face expressed shock and dismay.

"I'm not going to play baseball this year." His matter-of-fact, stern response held no hint of negotiating with me. My head dropped. I whimpered. My bottom lip protruded. A technique I learned from raising four boys.

"That's not gonna work, Grandma. I'm not playing this year." Nicholas stood his ground.

Since I loved the game of baseball, I played a few seasons of softball on René's women's team. A better term might be that I filled an open spot on the roster. Fewer balls are hit to right field, making it my position of choice – and the coach's choice for me. I didn't have strong legs for fast running. The balls I hit seldom made it to the outfield. After a few seasons I resorted to attending her games as a spectator.

As the boys were growing up, John and I wanted to teach them good sportsmanship and team spirit. We encouraged them in sports, which meant hours were spent on hard bleacher seats. All four sons wrestled when they were young. Unfortunately, with only a 15 month age gap between Larry and Stephen, they wrestled in the same weight category, often having to wrestle each other. One year, both the boys qualified to go to State. Both were eliminated from first, then eliminated for second. When it came to third place play offs, the final round came down to Larry and Stephen wrestling each other. The winner would qualify for Nationals.

"You go out there and wrestle as if it were a stranger. Don't think of it as your brother. You both wrestle to win!" I tried to encourage them knowing there would be heartbreak in the end. Larry advanced to Nationals, a trip to Antioch, California which included a visit to Magic Mountain, a theme park. When I couldn't find Larry after the match, I was told by a teammate that he was seen running around the track, in tears. The winner of the match was devastated when he eliminated his brother.

Larry, at age 18, went to England with an All-Conference football team. Larry, Chris and Duane played football in high school. Stephen played sports at a younger age but in his teens, though he attended all his brothers' games, he preferred to work in place of endless hours of football practice. He saved his money and his first vehicle was sitting in the driveway, bought and paid for, by the time he got his drivers license.

As adults, they continue to engage in various sports. Chris became a fourth-degree black belt and had his own martial arts studio for 10 years. He also enjoys running. Larry and Duane are runners, competing in 5k's, half-marathons, and marathons. Stephen bought his first home at age 21 and participates in motorized sports; owning a river boat, a ski boat, and numerous side-by-side vehicles.

Sean endures my baseball addiction with grace. He enjoys the sport but not to the degree I do. Every ball hit, every swing and miss, every stolen base or run crossing home plate, elicit an excited response, or groan, from me. If it's a slow, slow game, I multi-task. I'm good at that. Multi-tasking keeps me from wasting three hours of my day. *Wait... Wasting? Would watching baseball really be a waste?* Other than watching the Mariners play — or a Seahawks football game — you'll seldom find me in front of the television.

> *Baseball, it is said,*
> *is only a game. True.*
> *And the Grand Canyon*
> *is only a hole in the ground in Arizona.*

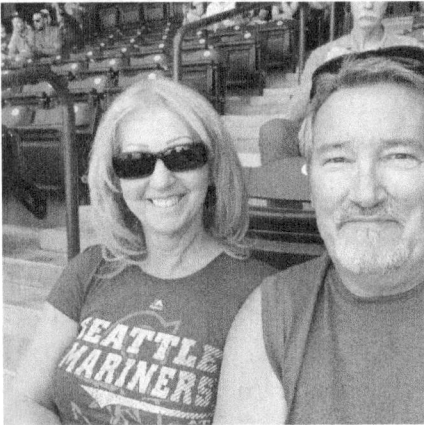

Me and Sean at a Mariners baseball game.

∞ ∞ ∞

∞ ∞ ∞

Bigger Pond - Smaller Fish

Sean and I were heartbroken when the owners of the waterfront home we rented on Anderson Island decided to sell. The $750,000 price tag was out of our budget. We bought a house inland. It was hard enough to move away from the waterfront but we were also devastated we no longer lived next to Jimmy and Joy Ng. Only two miles would separate us at our new location, but it felt like a significant distance considering our spontaneous get-togethers. We had a tradition of watching Seahawks football games on their big screen every Sunday, (or should I say we watched while Sean catnapped on their couch) and occasional Mariners baseball games in the spring and summer.

"Why don't you guys come over and watch the Mariners game with us?" Jimmy asked. We had just sat down to eat dinner, but Jimmy insisted, "Bring your plates over and eat here!" We did.

"We have four pork chops and only two mouths. Can you come over and help us out?" It was Joy calling this time.

Our houses were just a stone's throw away. When Jimmy and Joy's two grandkids needed daily transportation to Bellevue, Washington for a class, they drove them the hour-long distance, plus a ferry ride, every weekday. Sean and I volunteered to give them a break and take over the drive each Wednesday. We loved the affectionate name that the Ng grandchildren, Colin and Katie, gave us. We were virtual grandparents. Sean and I have always felt like part of the Ng family.

The home we bought was a lovely three bedroom, two bath,

single story home at the end of a secluded cul-de-sac. It was elegantly designed with teakwood floors, open floor plan and a large deck; it sat on a pie shaped lot with lush green lawn, apple trees, and surrounded by evergreens and privacy. Deer came to our front porch to be fed. But, we didn't have the sights and sounds of the water that gave the island that magical feel — and we didn't have the Ngs next door. The idea of moving back to Oregon frequently came to mind. Sean humored me:

"Give the island five years," he said. "If you want to leave after that, I'll happily go wherever you want to go."

In 2020, our friend, Mike Moore, who lived in southern California, invited us to join his family for their annual baseball spring training weekend in Arizona. Since we would already be in Arizona then, we graciously accepted. We had a wonderful time with nearly two dozen others who stayed at the mansion rented by the Moore family; three baseball games and an evening at Top Golf were on the list of activities during the four-day weekend. Sean and I had an additional two weeks to spend in Arizona after the others headed home. We purchased tickets to see one more Mariner game the following week. The game was canceled.

The COVID pandemic had struck; events were being canceled, businesses closed, employees were laid off, masks were required, and keeping a six-foot distance from others in public was enforced. We spent the remainder of our vacation hiking, keeping a distance between hikers we passed, lounging at the pool, and playing board games.

While listening to the news of COVID, I wondered how selling a house in the near future would be affected. *Will the housing market crash with people out of work?* Maybe now would be a good time to make the move to Oregon.

I spent several days thinking about it. I couldn't just spring the idea on Sean. With 19 years of singleness since I'd been widowed, I'd grown accustomed to having things my way. I knew I still had a tendency to want control. Now, I needed to consider his wishes as well. He loves the island. *What if he says no? Will I be content to stay on the island?*

The large poolside umbrella shaded us from Arizona's warm March sun as we played the board game, Ticket to Ride.

"Remember when we discussed moving to Oregon... some day?" My voice trailed off. Sean often joked that when I started a conversation with a question, he knew he was being forewarned.

"Yeeesss..." his voice hinted at *what's she up to now?*

"You said after five years on the island, if I want to move to Oregon, you would follow." He waited for me to continue. "Hear me out before you give me an answer. With COVID, everyone is getting laid off work. We don't know how that will affect the housing market. It's just short of five years. I'm wondering if we should try to sell the house and move before the housing market crashes? I really would like to be close to the kids and grandkids in Oregon."

I was surprised when Sean immediately dialed our realtor friend who had the house on the market before we returned from vacation. It sold quickly and by May we were enroute to Grants Pass, population 30,000 plus, where Sean knew my family and a few of my friends with whom he'd become acquainted. I wondered how he would adjust. He was well known on Anderson Island and accustomed to being the *Big Fish in a Small Pond.*

Sometimes, to grow, we must jump into a bigger pond.

Chapter Twenty

Being Grandpa

We purchased a home ideal for entertaining in Grants Pass. It was a five minute drive from Duane's family, and six miles from Stephen. Sean joined the Relics baseball team hoping to find his niche in the community. The niche didn't materialize there. We hiked many of the local trails, we played pickleball daily, but most importantly, we spent quality time with family.

When we married, Sean became an instant grandpa to my 15 grandchildren. One of our joys while we lived on the island was when eight-year-old Miles, who lived in Seattle, spent three or four days with us each summer; Grandparents' camp we called it. He kept us busy from morning to evening with pickleball, painting with Grandma, hiking, metal detecting, and watching Twilight Zone with Grandpa in the evenings. Shortly after Miles returned home from one such trip, Larry called me to share Miles' request after dinner:

"Dad, can we paint and watch Twilight Zone tonight?" He'd become accustomed to the routine while at our house.

Now, living in Oregon, we had the opportunity to spend quality time with Duane's children who were homeschooled. Dusti called one day with a request.

"I'm running out of ideas for electives for the kids. Would you two have anything you would like to teach?" Sean jumped at the opportunity. He loved theater and used to perform in the annual Christmas Revels in Tacoma. At one time he wrote a children's play which had been performed in local Tacoma area theaters. Sean suggested a drama class to Dusti. He rewrote his play *The Siblings Grimm* to accommodate fewer cast members. Children from three other homeschooled families joined the weekly rehearsals from October to December, culminating into a performance on stage at a local church. Grandpa Sean also gave ukulele lessons and held film festivals for them at our home.

Shirt given to Sean by the grandkids.

My grandson, Nicholas, a senior in high school when I first met Sean, formed an instant bond with him. Each year at Christmas, they exchanged gag gifts with one another. When he left for Virginia to attend college, his mother drove back with him, then she flew home. Three consecutive years, when the school term ended, Sean and I flew to Washington, D.C. and made the road trip back to Oregon with Nicholas — three different routes across the U.S. The first trip had Sean and Nicholas alternating, one driving while the other read aloud *The Hitchhiker's Guide to the Galaxy* trilogy while I rode in the back seat. They both seemed to thrive on slapstick humor. Nicholas finished the end of the third book.

"At last!" I raised my voice so they could hear me in the front seat, exaggerating a huge sigh. I would miss seeing the interaction between the two guys though, now that they finished the book.

"You can start the next book while I drive." Nicholas said to Sean.

"What next book? I thought you said it was a trilogy. You just finished the third book."

"That's the humor of the book! It's called a trilogy, but it has five books."

I groaned, loudly, as I hid my smile. I couldn't always hear what was being read, nor did I want to as that is not my choice of humor. But, watching and listening to them crack up in hysterics as they read, kept me amused.

Sean eventually found his niche in Grants Pass when we got involved with the local pickleball groups but most importantly, he became as much of a grandfather to my grandchildren as I am their grandma. I've learned to say *our* grandchildren... because they are.

The strength within me is fueled
by family and friends who help me
to navigate through challenging times.

∞ ∞ ∞

Yuma, Arizona

"**M**aybe we should do something different next year. I think I've had enough of Arizona for a while. Maybe we can go to Hawaii or some other location. What do you think?" I asked Sean. We were leaving Scottsdale, Arizona, enroute to Yuma to visit my longtime girlfriend, Sharon, and her husband, Jerry. After six years of vacationing in Arizona, I felt ready for a change of pace. Sean agreed. It was March 2021. Sharon and Jerry had been wanting us to visit them in Yuma. They spent time traveling in their RV during the summer and wintered in Yuma at a 55+ park.

"Why would anyone want to live in Yuma? It's not the end of the earth but you can see it from there!" Sean complained as we drove across Arizona. We arranged to spend a week in Yuma with them before heading back to Oregon. My friend, Robbie, planned to meet us in Yuma for the week. We rented a park model together. The Scottsdale/Phoenix area is lovely. Their desert landscape has an abundance of saguaros, prickly pear, barrel cacti and other vegetation, surrounded by red rock formations. As we neared Yuma, we saw less cacti, no saguaros, barren mountain ranges, and a lot of grayish-brown desert dirt. We were unimpressed.

When we arrived at Country Roads RV Village we were surprised to see the park beautifully landscaped with palm trees, ficus trees, and cacti. The gated community, home to 1,300 park models and RV lots, proved to be a snowbird's paradise; five swimming pools, four hot tubs, pickleball, volleyball and shuffleboard. For the artists, there are wood, pottery, and lapidary shops. Clubs included board games, card games, quilting, painting, creative writing, and so much more.

The retired residents appeared to be community oriented and friendly. We quickly noted that if you were bored, it was your own fault. Some call it "a cruise ship on land," or "a summer camp for seniors." Some even refer to it as "God's waiting room" since many retire and live there until the end of their lives.

"What does this place remind you of?" I asked Sean on our second day of visiting.

"Anderson Island," he responded without hesitation.

"Yes!" We loved Anderson Island for its small community feel. This park gave us that same feeling. On the third day, we made an offer on our vacation home. So much for having enough of Arizona!

"One thing it doesn't have is karaoke." Sean told our soon-to-be new neighbor, Brenda McKey.

"Well start it!" she said. That's all Sean needed to hear. One of the incentives I used in my suggestion of moving to Oregon was maybe he could start his own karaoke business. Once there, we discovered there were so many venues in local bars that he chucked the idea.

Karaoke on the island, being in a restaurant, was a family affair. The bar is at the back end of the restaurant where patrons can participate in karaoke without a bar atmosphere. We didn't find that in Grants Pass. Sean would attend without me occasionally since I didn't enjoy the bar scene. I preferred our karaoke nights at home with friends.

Kim and Eddie, the prior island karaoke jockeys, had left the island, hosting at other South Sound locations. Ron Forest, of Black Hat Karaoke, now hosts at the Lakeshore. We gave serious consideration to the karaoke business idea as we drove back to Oregon. Arriving home, Sean called Ron, who agreed to be his mentor. In no time, Sean was ordering equipment. We mirrored Ron's setup. Sean scheduled dates with the activities office at Country Roads to host karaoke throughout the snowbird season, October through April. We would spend Spring and Summer at home in Grants Pass.

That summer we became familiar with the equipment. Sean was in heaven! We had professional equipment in our home. Friends and family came over for karaoke nights. We hosted a patio party at Robbie's house. By the time we returned to Country Roads in October for the snowbird season, we were comfortable with the process. Karaoke nights at Country Roads were a success from the first event on October 8, 2021. We schedule the events two weeks apart throughout the snowbird season. During warmer temperatures we are on the patio outside the ballroom. When December and January's evening temperatures turn chilly, we host in the huge ballroom. The numbers continued to grow. At one event, I counted 250 people.

"Bring your own drinks and snacks, and your singing voice," we told people, "No admission, but tips are accepted." Country Roads has a large population of dancers so we leave ample room for dancing when we set up on the large community patio.

"Where else can you go, not have to spend money on a meal or drinks, and enjoy an evening of singing — or listening to others sing — dance, socialize, have a good time, and not worry about getting a 'driving under the influence' ticket when you go home in your golf cart, or on your bike?" It is something I love to point out to people when we advertise our karaoke events.

A year after buying our house in Grants Pass, Duane sprung the news on us.

"I'm not running for another term as state representative next year. We're going to sell the house and move to Texas." That meant Larry lived in the Seattle area, Stephen lived in Grants Pass, Chris lived in the Portland area, and now Duane's family would be living in Texas. The older grandchildren were in, or out of college and lived in other scattered places.

Since we loved Arizona, Sean and I decided to sell our Oregon home and make Arizona our permanent residence. We bought a second home in Country Roads, more conducive to full time living. We kept the first house as a rental. By selling our large house in Oregon, we are free to travel when Arizona's summers reach highs of 120 degrees. During the moderately warm winter — peak season for snowbirds — we stay active with volleyball, pickleball, karaoke events, and entertaining friends in our home.

Sean and me - pickleball

"What is it you enjoy about karaoke?"we are frequently asked. Our philosophy is that it takes courage to stand in front of an audience to sing. I experienced that fear for a long time. Now, like Sean, I love to see new singers take that step of courage, risk the chance of possible humiliation, and experience the joy of singing to an audience. Music is in our soul. We wake in the night with a song in our head. We hear a tune during the day that becomes an ear worm. We listen to music to lift our spirits. To be able to express that music through singing is an additional bonus in our lives. We like to say that *Karaoke with KJ Sean and Esther* is our opportunity to fling joy at others. We have a fun tradition to help break-the-ice for first-time singers. The loud *clang, clang, clang* of a large gold cowbell gets the crowd's attention. Then Sean announces,

"Ladies and gentlemen, we have a virgin in the house! Tonight she (he) is going to lose her (his) karaoke virginity right here in front of all of you!" The crowd applauds wildly, cheering for the first-time singer. The crowd knows it's a difficult step that is being taken. Many of them have taken that same step, while others succumb to their fear, hoping to someday be the one for whom the bell tolls. "Someday I'll get up there," they tell me.

Once the karaoke virgin loses that singing virginity, they are awarded a fun little gift: a silly pair of flashing led glasses, or a pair of John Lennon style horn-rimmed sunglasses, or another trivet of some type. Typically, they will be back singing at the next event.

We have volunteered our karaoke services at the local Arizona State Veterans Home and at several assisted living facilities. There, it becomes more of a concert, entertaining the residents, but we incorporate a lot of sing-a-longs to get everyone involved.

Many professional singers opt not to listen to karaoke singing.

"Karaoke isn't for everyone. Some find it painful to listen to a nervous, or maybe a tone-deaf singer. That's ok," I tell them. "Karaoke is meant for those who don't have the opportunity to sing professionally on stage. It's a chance for them to have three minutes of fame performing for an audience. An opportunity they may never have otherwise."

Karaoke is a process of overcoming fears, learning to enjoy the music within us, and singing until our heart's content.

*Music can heal the wounds
that medicine cannot touch. -
Debasish Mridha*

∞ ∞ ∞

Sean and me singing at karaoke.

Me and Sean in Yuma, Arizona.

∞∞∞

Perfect For Me

Sean and I are extremely happy in our community, playing sand volleyball two hours, five to six days of the week during the winter season. We hold game nights and movie days at our home, and play pickleball. We take dance lessons, attend (and volunteer to help at) tribute concerts and live-band dances. Our karaoke nights are one of the most attended events in the park. My retirement is more than I'd ever dreamed it would be. I'm thankful I took that risk and hit "send" when I saw Sean's profile on the dating site. Though Sean and I get along well and are equally yoked in many ways, we do have our differences:

Sean needs his daily naps. I feel like I'm going to miss something important if I take time for a nap. He's an early bird - I'm a night owl. Our tastes in music and movies differ as well. Sean reads everything. I read headlines. He watches a movie in silence. I like to predict what's going to happen in every scene. He's deadline oriented. I'm project oriented.

"The trash is getting pretty full." I hint at the actions he should take. He translates the necessary actions, and to the best of my knowledge, he deciphers the comment as, *I need to take that out by midnight tonight.*

Sean loves to cook, trying new recipes. We take turns cooking. I decide the menu on days he cooks; I tell him what we're having, he looks up a recipe and provides us with a wonderful meal. He is the messiest cook I know. I follow him around, cleaning up after him. My early restaurant training taught me to be a clean-as-you-go person. Sean always uses exact ingredients; he measures everything. I like to cook simple meals. I substitute ingredients. I measure with a pinch of this and a dash of that. I will admit, having him cook for me is worth cleaning up after him.

Sean is always hot. I'm always cold. I recently ordered a sweatshirt that states: "Yes, I'm cold. Me: 24:7." Sean tells people he used to get excited when he snuggled against me during the night and I'd respond, "You're hot!". His bubble burst when he realized I meant *move over, your body is too warm.* The heat of his body ignites the dreaded hot flashes.

We both have quirks that could drive the other one crazy, if we let them. I'm sure Sean rolls his eyes behind those sunglasses more often than he lets on. I like to think I'm the perfect wife because he treats me as if I am. He is less verbal about things than I am. Sometimes it takes a lot of work on my part, keeping my years of independence in check. Our many cultural differences have helped us to broaden each other's interests. I now attend plays in theaters, he occasionally listens to, and sings, country music. He once convinced me to watch the musical, *Hello Dolly!* and asked me what I thought.

"The plot was good, but it would have been much better without all that singing and dancing." The next theater event we attended was John Steinbeck's *Of Mice and Men.* I loved the play. I asked Sean what he thought.

"The plot was good, but it would have been better if it had some singing and dancing." We compromise and we negotiate. We've learned to appreciate that it's ok to have separate interests as well as the many similar interests we share.

We both love to socialize but Sean is more outgoing than I am. I must be careful not to slip back into my old comfort zones. When we are invited to go places, I sometimes balk at going.

"I don't really know anybody there. It's going to be uncomfortable."

"You always say that but once you're there, you enjoy it," Sean reminds me. I know he's right, but fighting the desire to opt out, I snip at him,

"Fine! I'll go." — I'm always glad I did.

———

Our long road trip in the summer of 2023 took us to Oregon, Washington, Colorado, Texas, Florida, back to Texas and then home to Arizona. During our trip we spent a week on Anderson Island staying in our friends' guest cottage. We hiked down to the beach where Sean had proposed. Our anniversary would soon be approaching. Arriving at the shoreline Sean asked,

"Should I get on my knee and propose again?"

"Are you sure you'd get the same answer from me?" I raised my eyebrow in question.

"Hmmmm, maybe I'll just look for agates," he said. We laughed. Of course I would say "yes" again. We have so much fun together. I wouldn't trade him for a million bucks — but please don't tempt me with two million. *He's not perfect, but he's perfect for me!*

Years ago, I found a small plastic card in a gift shop titled Back Seat Driver's License. I still have it. I keep it in the console of the car. It's a skill I've become good at. It gets better with each trip.

"Whoa!" I flinched. "Can you slow down a little sooner when you come up behind a car?"

"The car will automatically slow down before we get too close." I felt the roll of his eyes behind his dark glasses. Regardless, his voice remained calm, dismissing my concern. He loves to use the self-driving feature on the cruise control. I do not trust that feature.

"Well, can you start braking a little sooner, before the car makes its decision?" An 8,500 mile, 10-week road trip in a Honda CRV with my husband has perfected my back seat driving skills. When I'm driving, I know if I'm in control of the car or not. If he's driving, I can only speculate.

"That truck's gonna pull out up there."

"I see it."

"I wasn't sure."

Sean's driving lessons started on our first date in Oregon. I asked him to slow the Miata down when taking the curves too fast for my comfort. Nine years later, he's still undergoing my training program. His favorite seems to be when I ask....

"Why did you park here?"

Sean scuffs his feet when he walks. I told him he sounds like a 90 year-old shuffling his feet. Early into our dating I asked him,

"Didn't your mother ever teach you how to pick up your feet?"

"Yes, but my legs are too long." He says he thinks he picked up the habit as a child because he loved hearing the sound of the taps on the bottom of his shoes when he scuffed his heels.

The first indication I had of Sean's emotional side came shortly after we got engaged. It was almost Christmas when I visited him on the island. He dug out a DVD he wanted me to watch. *Amal and the Night Visitors* is about a crippled poor boy and his mother who are visited by the three wise men following the Star of Bethlehem. At this point, Sean wasn't aware of the fact that I didn't like black and white movies, musicals, or operas. *Amal and the Night Visitors* is a combination of all three. Five minutes into the movie, as the introductory music still played, I heard him sniffling. I looked over to see him reaching for the Kleenex box. His crumpled face had tears streaming down his cheeks.

"Why are you crying? Nothing's happened yet." I had not seen this side of him. His voice cracked as he answered.

"But I know what's gonna happen." He wiped his tears and blew his nose. I cry when I'm happy, when I'm sad, when I see other people crying. I've always said, "I cry at the drop of a dime," — but Sean, he can cry at the drop of a penny. I've learned to expect the emotional side to show up during most movies. When friends come over to watch a movie, they ask if we have an ample supply of tissue for Sean.

"What they don't understand," Sean explains, "is that it's not just sad movies that make me cry. It's when something emotionally touching happens."

Sean is a wonderful storyteller. I suppose that may come from his being a journalist for many years. While we were in Seattle with my son one evening, he participated in the Moth Storytelling night. He took first place. When listening to a storyteller, you get to hear all the little details that make up the story. Sean doesn't know how to tell a short story. When the opportunity arrives for him to tell a particular story – that I've heard 100 times by now – I often suggest,

"Can you tell the short version?" I smile and wink at the recipient, giving them a heads up that this is going to be a long one.

"I don't know any short version." Sean's response never surprises me. He proceeds with the long version.

Meeting someone for the first time, Sean is predictable in introducing me.

"This is my current wife, Esther." It always gets the same response.

"Current wife?" They give him a confused laugh, not quite understanding his intention. I confirm for them.

"He's not sure how long I'm going to stick around." I shrug and laugh. When we share stories with others about our life adventures, Sean often states,

"I'm still in her training program."

"And at the rate he progresses, he will never graduate," I say.

Sean's humor is raw but I'm fortunate that he has one. When we travel, I prefer to be the passenger but I do, on occasion, take my turn driving. Once, while I reluctantly took my turn, Sean fell asleep. Head back, mouth gaping, chin nearly touching his chest. His phone was within reach. *I have to do it!* I carefully lifted the phone from his lap and tapped the camera button, held it up and took a picture of him. I knew the first thing he'd do when he woke up would be to open his phone to read the news. Being a career journalist, he says, "News is always happening. It changes by the minute."

When he woke up, as I predicted, he picked up his phone. I

stifled my giggles. His head spun to face me, giving me the evil eye. I erupted in laughter.

"I couldn't resist!" It made my driving duty worth the disruption of my leisure travel time. I would never be the one to post that picture to Facebook. Sean on the other hand, doesn't have a bashful bone in his body.

"My wife has too much fun at my expense!" the caption read under the posted photo. — And I do. — In my defense, when he says that, I respond with...

"But he gives me so much material to work with!"

This is a guy where numerous times I've seen him looking for something.

"What are you looking for?" Most times I can find the item for him.

"My sunglasses." He sounds frustrated at losing them... again.

"They're on your face!" Or "Check the top of your head."

"I knew that," is his normal response. I roll my eyes and laugh because I love that about him. Yes, he gives me lots of material to work with. And, since I'm the one writing this book, he doesn't have the opportunity to share the many stories I'm sure he'd like to divulge about me.

Sean has survived numerous near-death experiences, although not by my hands. Three such experiences include a small plane crash, cancer, and sepsis.

"That convinces me I'm immortal and I'll outlive you." He tells me as if it's a matter of fact. I'm not convinced.

"You won't outlive me. If I go first, I'm taking you with me! You'd never know how to do anything if I'm not here to tell you!"

With that in mind, I am confident we will live the rest of our lives together. I'm amazed he survived the 64 years of life before we met.

I asked Sean to read through my story to make sure I used the proper words, in the proper places. He's a word guy and is particular about that. After reading it, he told me there was one issue he found —

"Nowhere does the word *magnificent* appear before my name."

Maybe I'll accept the two million now.

I've found that growing up means
being honest about what I want,
what I feel, what I need, and who I am.

∞∞∞

From the Shadows
to the Spotlight

D uring our 2023 summer visit to the Pacific Northwest, we attended karaoke night at the Elks Lodge in Lakewood. The karaoke jockeys were our friends, Kim and Eddie. After I'd belted out a playful song by K.T. Oslin, *Do Ya,* Eddie gave me a huge hug and commented:

"Esther, you've come a long way!" His words spread an overall warmth of pleasure throughout my body. Of course, he meant I'd come a long way in my singing ability, as he recalled my early-stage performances. But that phrase meant more than that to me. It made me reflect on my entire life. Eddie was right. I have come a long way — in more ways than one!

With one step at a time, I moved outside of my comfort zone — outside my fragile, frail existence — I stepped beyond the dark shadows of my fears and my shyness. Now, I can honestly answer that officer's question of so many years ago,

"Yes, I am ok!"

There comes a time when the chapter ends, you turn the page, and close the book, for now.

The End

∞∞∞

∞ ∞ ∞

Epilogue

My sons grew to be upstanding citizens in spite of the ups and downs of our household environment, and the loss of their father. They, and their wives, have blessed me with an abundance of grandchildren ranging from biological, adopted, step-grandchildren, and foster grandchildren.

Larry has devoted 25 years to curing cancer. He says it won't be cured in his lifetime, but he stood on strong shoulders to help improve the quality of life for cancer patients, and he hopes the next generation can stand on his.

Stephen Stark Excavation, LLC. was started more than 20 years ago by Stephen and his wife, René. His good reputation kept their head above water during the 2007 housing crisis, when housing (and excavation work) nearly came to a halt. Their business is still thriving today.

Christopher opened Stark's TaeKwonDo studio in 2004. He is a Fourth Degree Black Belt, holds numerous certificates to teach special training programs in self defense, training police officers and security personnel. He operated his own studio for over 10 years before changing to a career in security.

Duane became a pastor, an Oregon state representative, and in 2023, with his wife, Dusti, he co-founded Fostering Bridges, a non-profit organization located in East Texas. They have a mixed family of biological, adopted, and foster children.

All have made their mama proud.

Me: I am living the retired life I could only have dreamed of so many years ago. I'm thankful I took the steps I did to overcome my fears and to gain confidence in myself.

The Stark Boys - 2015
Stephen, Duane, Christopher and Larry

Your Comfort Zone Challenge

Every day... ask yourself _"What can I do today to stretch my comfort zone?"_ Then take action. It might be:

Say hello to everyone you pass on the street.
Make a phone call to someone.
Stop by and meet a neighbor,
...or try a dance class (or other sport).

REMEMBER: **Every step** you take, even if it's a tiny baby step, will stretch that comfort zone and put you one step closer to the joy you seek in life.

Keep taking those steps, no matter how big or small, and you will get there! .

Read the encouraging quotes at the end of the book, and keep re-reading them if you need the reminders.

My prayer is that you break through the barriers that hold you back!

∞∞∞

Notes

THANK YOU for reading my book! I'm grateful for your support. As an author, I rely on readers like you to help spread the word about my work. **Reviews are a crucial part of the book-buying process, and your honest feedback would be a huge help.**

To leave a review, please follow these steps.

1. Go to Amazon and type "Esther Stark book" in the search bar.

2. Click on the link to my *YOU Were Shy?* book.

3. Scroll down to the "Reviews" section at the bottom of the page.

4. Click the "Write a Review" button and share your thoughts.

Your review will only take a few minutes, but it will make a big difference in helping me reach more readers. Thank you again for your time and support!

A Special Note

To my Daughters-in-Law

A special thank you for the joy you've brought into the lives of my sons and to the Stark family. I never worried about having a daughter of my own. I knew with four boys, I'd one day have daughters too. Each of you have filled that role in my life. There are a few of you who no longer bear the Stark name but you bore the wonderful grandchildren I have in my life... and you still hold a spot in my heart. *Thank you!*

To My Grandchildren

I didn't name each of you in this book but you all hold a piece of my heart, and I love you more than you'll ever know. I have such wonderful memories about each of you. Sometimes a story pops into my mind and I just smile. I'm amazed and so proud to see the wonderful men and women you are all becoming.

"As a parent (grandparent), we are only as happy as our saddest child."

Contact Information

If you have been encouraged by reading this book, please leave a review on Amazon and feel free to drop me a note at the email below. I'd love to hear from you.

Contact Esther Stark at:

email: youwereshy.author@gmail.com

On Facebook at:

Paint with Esther

Karaoke with KJ Sean and Esther (Facebook page)

References

The Five Love Languages by Gary Chapman can be found in most bookstores. He has a full series of love language books relating to husband and wife, children, and a single's edition.

How to Win Friends and Influence People by Dale Carnegie can be found on Amazon in paperback and kindle, and is available in most bookstores.

I'm unable to locate sources for *Speak Up* and *7 Ancient Ways to Happiness*.

Encouraging Quotes

The best way to predict your future is to create it.
  -Abraham Lincoln

You must be willing to give up what you are, to become what you want to be. - Orrin Woodward

Life will only change when you become more committed to your dreams than you are to your comfort zone.

There are no secrets to success. It is reached through preparation, hard work, and learning from failure.

The journey of a thousand miles begins with one small step.

Don't watch life from the sidelines, participate in it.

Self confidence is a journey. It doesn't happen overnight.

In any given moment we have two options: to step forward into growth or step backward into safety.

Stop being afraid of what can go wrong and start getting excited about what can go right.

The greatest investment you will ever make is investing in yourself.

It's a slow process but quitting won't speed it up.

When things change inside you, things change around you.

Breathe, darling. This is just a chapter, not your whole story.   -- S.C. Louric

You can't create the next chapter in your life if you keep re-reading the last one.

If you can change your mind, you can change your life.

If you can't fly, run. If you can't run, walk. If you can't walk, crawl, but whatever you do, you have to keep moving forward. – Martin Luther King Jr.

Success is sometimes the outcome of a whole series of failures. – VanGogh

Never make a permanent decision on a temporary emotion.

Promise me not to hide yourself when you are in pain. It's unfair that we laughed together but you cried alone.

Just when the caterpillar thought her life was over, she began to fly.

Rock bottom became the solid foundation from which I built my life.

Look in the mirror each day and rather than say, "I think I can, I think I can" ... start saying "Yes, I can! Yes, I can."

Most of all ----- **Have faith in yourself. You deserve it!**

∞ ∞ ∞

Made in the USA
Monee, IL
09 February 2025